I0846442

THE UNDERGROUND VAULT

AN UNDERGROUND HIP-HOP MONTHLY

First Printing, 2023
The Underground Vault
Printed with Amazon Kindle Direct Publishing.
www.TheUndergroundVault.com
Cover art by C DYER ART & DESIGN.

VOLUME 1: ISSUE 7: July 2023

CONTENTS

RAP

Napoleon Da Legend has over the past five or six years, cemented himself as an absolute favourite. The emcee, heralding from Paris / New York / D.C, has released dozens of albums - each crafted into unique bodies of work. Built on personal experience, fandom and passion. His two most recent out puts include an album entirely done in his native language - French - called, *Le Dernier Glacier [The Last Glacier]*, as well as an album entirely produced and compiled by **Beat Junkies** extraordinaire **D-Styles**. The Beat Junkie-produced album, titled *Invincibl Rap Mislz* is one of my favourite albums of the year. The song, *Wu-Styles,* made it to #1 in my favourite songs mid-year. This conversation aims to capture the story behind these latest additions in NDL's discography, with a focus on the D-Styles joint. **Enjoy**.

MISLZ

TUV: Let us begin with the French album. That I found absolutely fascinating. You put out an album a couple months ago called *The Last Glacier*, or at least the French variant of that, and it's essentially an entire album done in French. Is French your first language or second language?

NDL: Technically French is my first language as I was born in Paris and both of my parents are from the Comoros Islands in Lower East Africa. I came to America when I was four, so English kind of replaced French because I started speaking English a lot more. More fluently than French.

TUV: What took you this long to put out an album in French? Perhaps I'm wrong but I've never heard a French NDL album before this.

NDL: Yeah, I mean, that was the first time I did anything in French entirely. I had done little things here or there, a year or two ago. But that kind of prompted me to be like, "you know, let me try to do a whole album in French." Basically, I had gone on tour in 2017 in Europe to a lot of French speaking countries and I built relationships with people over there. So I started practicing the language again, speaking it… And later on, I just wanted to try. I had done an interview also in French – a video interview – and the interview went viral. It had like 200-250,000 views in a few days. I realized, that this was kind of crazy, just because I spoke French on it. So I tried to do a song a few months later and I liked it.

I got invited by the top French rapper of all time, **Akhenaton** from the group **IAM**, to be on his album. He asked me to be on one song where we do one version where he raps in French and I rap in English, and then another version where we flip it around. And we kept working. He produced three albums in English for me. And we also made other music. We did a single, *Rétroviseur* where we rapped in French. I'm like, "I'm rapping in French with the most legendary rapper there is over there… right?" And I enjoyed doing it. It was just another challenge for me. Since I grew up and lived in America since the age of four, to speak on my story in French – an American story in French – French rappers have done a million stories about their lives in France or Africa, other countries… but no one did it like "yo, I lived in America my whole life." It just had value to doing something like that.

TUV: Do you feel like it is more of a challenge when it comes to writing? I imagine writing raps is always going to be puzzle solving – this is a new kind of puzzle, right?

NDL: It's not just writing, it's also spitting and saying it – making it sound natural. Making you feel it. Learning how… It's like learning how to drive. You go from driving a car that's easy to drive and then you go to driving an 18-wheeler. You still know how to drive because you know how to rap – you know how you want it to sound and flow – but it's just a different mind state. It just took me a little while to learn how to master it and fine tune it. Something that would take me no time in English, took me a lot more time in French. In my head, I just wanted to put a project out like that. It's not like I'm looking to have others – I just wanted to have one, and then come back to what I do.

TUV: You're one of those artists that puts out a shit ton of projects – but also – the projects that you do, they always have a slightly different angle. It'll be on a specific show that you're into – a particular concept – it'll be with a certain producer that will curate a specific sound… every project ends up being a little bit different. It feels as though each project is a stand alone, isolated project, that allows you to be cre-ative in a new way. At a point, it seemed like, "oh shit, you doing a French project… that's like an extension of that philosophy…"**

NDL: Yeah, it's kind of like if you ever watched a Netflix series like *Black Mirror*. Everything is a theme. Futurism, technology, its effect on humanity… but every episode is a stand alone. It's a different universe you're going into. Well, I will have a few projects that will link up – including a triple album that I have coming out which will be all linked – but for the most part, I just go into a zone and explore that zone. Whether it's a producers beats, or a series, it'll be a theme… Like Afro-Street, hip-hop and afrobeat fusion, and I'll just go into that and see what I come up with.

TUV: I always look forward to an NDL project because it's not just 'another NDL project.' It is it's own piece of art within your catalogue. Every one of them stands out.

NDL: I don't like to be predictable. I just try to make the music and see what it's going to do. I think it's probably more of a risk – because a lot of people will prefer one over the other, but it's still me. It's still me rhyming, it's still my voice, it's still me talking about my life – just in different ways.

TUV: I want to transition to talking about this new *Invincibl Rap Mislz* project with D-Styles. I have a feeling, and you can correct me if I'm wrong, that this story starts a bit before this album. I interviewed Substance810 when he put out his album with D-Styles, and that album blew me away. The song you were on together, blew me away. I heard the album for the first time with a friend of mine. We planned out a night, got together, and listened to the

album together for the first time. Now this friend, he likes rap music, but he doesn't know all the characters... I told him though, "wait for the NDL track..." Cause I knew that you could bring that hard shit. You work well with that big, grandiose, epic style production, and the album – up until that point – was going in that direction. When the song came on though – it was a completely different vibe. It was more personal. It was story driven... It was slightly more sombre – but it still had that cinematic landscape... And the song fucked both of us up. I didn't know that just a couple months later we would be listening to a full album by D-Styles and yourself. Can you talk about how this joint came together – and am I correct in saying that it has something to do with that Substance810 joint?

NDL: Yeah, yeah! You're actually correct. I think it was **Substance**, we had been in touch. I'm not sure if it's him or D-Styles, one or the other hit me up to get on a song. He had the concept and I just followed in that vein. Cause I could easily find things in my life that had to do with that concept. So the story was very much drawn from real experiences.

TUV: Aint it Funny.

NDL: I remember that was the first time D-Styles was giving me feedback, like, "yo, man..." He was already telling me he was feeling what I was doing, but he was like, "yo, you adapt super well to any different sound. A lot of rappers don't adapt to different things as well as you do." We just kind of had that link. I think I was interviewed by the Beat Junkies which is D-Styles and **Rhettmatic** on their show, and after the show D-Styles was like, "yo, I'd like to send you some beats if you're open to it!" And I was like, "hell yeah." So he started sending me instrumentals, and we started building. We already knew that it was probably going towards a whole project together at that point.

TUV: What does the Beat Junkies and Invinsible Skratch Picklez mean to you? You're a hip-hop head, you're well versed in terms of the history of the culture. Both of these are really iconic groups – what does that mean to you?

NDL: I remember back in the day, me and one of my boys, I have several friends who were hip-hop heads, and we would just dive into different rabbit holes. I remember listening to... back in the day we were listening to **Souls of Mischief** and some of the things like that. Some of the shit on the west coast like **Freestyle Fellowship**... And he actually introduced me to turntablism. I knew what a DJ was. I knew what scratching was from hearing it on a record, but he had videos and it was actually videos of the **Invisible Skratch Picklez**. And we was just at awe. And to be honest with you, I didn't remember really who was who in those videos, but that really was my first memory of like, "wow, what are these guys doing with these records?" Like beat juggling and stuff like that, like, "Yo, this is incredible!"

When it came to the Beat Junkies, I knew a lot of them individually. I had heard of course **DJ Babu**, and Rhettmatic, and all of them individually. I was like, "this whole crew, encompassing all these ill dudes into one! And they're west coast!" I had never met them physically but I knew what their position in hip-hop history was. I knew how they impacted the culture. So I was ready. I knew that I was dealing with a staple. To me, to be dealing with people that are in a crew who are a staple in hip-hop culture? That's amazing to me in myself. Look, I came into this as a fan. Just somebody who loves hip-hop and started rhyming with his friends just like that. There aren't any other ambitions. And now to be like, "I'm actually working with one of these dudes…" I had to tell D-Styles, "yo! I used to watch ya'll videos back in the days and never never would I have thought that we would just be sitting there creating and putting something out to the public together."

TUV: It's amazing, considering the status of D-Styles, it's incredible to see him still actively working on music. But also, be tuned in enough that he's producing and curating joints for new cats, cats that weren't around when during his come up.

We talk about people like Muggs, but I think cats like Architect and D-Styles need to be within those same conversations. A lot of times that formula doesn't work out. You have a lot of OGs and veterans, and they don't always hit as 'hard' – they don't always feel so contemporary. A lot of dope work, dope to throw on and vibe out too – but often not really making a significant impression come the end of that calendar year. I think both the album that D-Styles did with Substance, and the one he did with you, carried that weight. The fact that he's been able to create such work decades after his rise, is incredible.

NDL: Yeah, I kind of have my theory on that. D-Styles, just dealing with him, and we really connected too… we've had our phone conversations, and they're important sometimes. Because every project is made differently. You work with different producers but your relationship with the producer is not necessarily the same. Some of it is just straight, with the distance of the internet, "I'll send you some beats, do what you do." But with him, there's a level of authenticity and I don't mean that in a cliché, but I think he does it for the right reasons, where a lot of projects aren't always

Invisibl Skratch Piklz

done for the right reasons. And sometimes you might or might not even realize that you're doing it. If tomorrow, somebody with a big name that you're a big fan of, asks you to do something, you might have an inkling to do it. You might want to do it, like "I'm a big fan, why not?" But I think, and I haven't asked him, but it seems like he has a reason why he selects certain people to work with. I think for me, he kept repeating that. That's why I think the project that we have is a little bit distinct than the stuff he's done with the other emcees, because he gave me instrumentals that others would have turned down or wouldn't have picked because they aren't run of the mill. And I think that's what he knew about me. I was able to really catch an emotion rather than having to sound like a certain image. We're in a very image driven industry and culture – hip-hop and rap – and a lot of rappers that you hear, it sounds hard, this is dark... this is this and that, and me? I love the craft of rap. I love a dark beat and a hard beat, don't get me wrong, but I also love a beat that just sounds... celestial. I like a beat that sounds like heavenly, and with a lot of light on it too. And I'm not scared of going to different tempos. Real slow or real fast, or everything in between. And I think that had to do with his decision for working with me.

And me, I just knew that he had some dope beats. I knew the scratches were going to be next level. And I knew that the creativity is going to be next level. Cause I had heard his *Phantazmagorea* album and I'm sure there were other albums done by turntablists but I had never heard anything quite like that before. So I knew that from a creative standpoint, I could push my pen far. When you were work with other people who have a narrow vision, and that's all you can expect that project to go is where that narrow vision is, and I'm not one to limit myself when it comes to creativity.

TUV: I think that appreciation for turntablism is really felt on the album. Like on the Substance album for instance, if we just kind of take the two in isolation, on the Substance record, there's cuts and scratches on there, but at the core of it – it's an album with incredibly dope cinematic beats, and dope raps. Now on here, on *Invincibl Rap Misslz,* the role of turntab-

lism is really emphasized. The most extreme example is the last cut, *Wu-Masters* which is one of my favourite joints of the year, but it's exactly that. It's you and him going back and forth. He throws out a classic Wu-line / sample, and you respond in dialogue. It's like an emcee duo who are trading bars back and forth, but you're there rapping with all of the Wu-Tang Clan! I love it. Let's pause on *Wu-Masters*. How did that come together? It's one of the coolest, creative, fun, but one of the dopest and hardest rap shit I've ever heard.

NDL: I appreciate it man. That idea came from me. That's what I'm saying in that I felt comfortable to bring ideas to the table. There's sometimes where you're confined to what it is, but we were already working on stuff and that's something that I requested. He didn't send me that beat, there were no instrumentals... I just had this idea one day. Like, I'm a big **Wu** fan. A lot of us are, if you're a fan of hip-hop... And I'm like, "how can I do a song, kind of like... showing that love to Wu but not like anybody else has done it in the past," and I love going back and forth... And I would love to go back and forth with every single member of the Wu-Tang Clan. So I told him, "I wanna do something where I go back and forth, but I want it to be every single one. It doesn't mean that everybody has to be equally presented, but I want to make sure that every member has his voice on it and I'm going back and forth." And a few days later, he just composes this beat... and which is crazy, because a lot of his beats were more on the slow side naturally, but this one was a real fast pace which actually was perfect for it because it was dynamic... it had no reason to get boring or anything... And I didn't even write what I put down, know what I mean? Things were laid down and I just recorded, and just went through it, a few times, to try to see where I could fit it, and just did it like that. So it was a new way for me to even make a song, which was exciting for me. I could only entrust D-Styles to produce something like that. Not every producer is capable of conceptualizing something like that.

TUV: Wait, were the cuts chosen before you ended up laying down the vocals?

NDL: Yeah, because I would have to fit in between that. Cause I was writing…, like "what's the definition of a real emcee… that would be me!" It was just a whole exercise man… Like if I was in the room with every Wu-Tang member, like "you say this, I say this." Just do it like that.

TUV: It was so much fun. Just being able to listen and pick up on all the references. And there was digging involved too! Like we know D-Stylez has these crates, but he's pulling from like GZA's verse from the Jedi Mind track *On the Eve of War*… or Cappadonna records, like "I came to the fork in the road and went straight…" and you as a fan, you know where that line leads – "from the crack vial to the golden gate!" But you give your own twist on it. And with every line structured like that, it's just fun. Real fun. And it sounds good! Somehow an idea that chaotic and crazy – fucking worked… Incredible job man.

NDL: Thank you. And like me, I'm a legitimate – grew up on Wu-tang – Wu-head. I felt like, not to sound arrogant, but I felt like I have my place in it, because I understand that whole world. It kind of bred me through the years through a distance.

TUV: When you put out a project with this kind of name status. A project with this much hype. Do you see these projects as stepping stones to something greater? Do you see the dividends paying off by doing a joint with say D-Styles? Or do you feel them as just another one of your albums within the catalogue? Move on. Do the next thing… kind of thing?

NDL: The way I do it, and the way I approach life, every one of them I put a lot of importance to it. I try to express something really authentic in every one of these albums. A lot of them, I'm doing them at the same time. Meaning I might be working with D-Styles at the same time where I was doing songs for *Buckets* with **Giallo Point** a few month earlier when I was working with the French album, probably waiting for some feature verses here and there, and producing that… So I work on songs individually, but then, like I said, D-Styles is a dude who does a lot of post-production. So whatever you send him, just like when I was doing *The World Changed* with **Amerigo [Gazaway]**, for like six months I hadn't heard from him and then he comes back and the album… there's cuts on it, there's skits, it was the same thing with D-Styles, there were cuts that weren't there when I did the song, there were little skits, things like that… And now that it's out, after I finished doing it, if I have another project on the go, I just focus on that. I can't be too result based because I'm living… What I do, is like an artisan. It's like an artisan beer or a wine. From a little patch of land on my region. Like, "this is that Napoleon Da Legend sound." I'm not Anheuser-Busch, when you're drinking Budweiser it's going to be on every single store in the world, it's going to be on billboards, it's going to be on TV, this and that… You gotta love this hip-hop the way we do it. This underground hip-hop. You gotta know who I am or the world that I'm in. I just keep going because I got more land to take. All of these albums, it is a step up. It is a landmark. More people discover who I am, more people

discover my sound. Some people may have heard of me in the past, but now they're like, "I understand what's up with this guy." I think it takes time for people. Some people might not get it the first time. I use different types of words. Different types of imagery. I'm not saying the same thing that a lot of rappers are saying. And a lot of people, that might throw them off, if they don't listen to that type of rhyme. I have a certain aesthetic.

So everything is moving towards where I belong. Time will tell. It's just an adventure. I'm journaling my life this whole time and it's just a big long verse and I keep writing it. It's not about quantity. To be honest with you, I got caught up in that whole COVID whirlwind where I was working on a lot of different things, and I just didn't stop. It's not like, "every year I gotta have this amount of albums," it's like, "right now, this is the amount of work I'm putting in." Look, I still have albums coming out this year and I've been on tour the last month. So I haven't recorded a single song and music still comes out. This is just an accumulation of work. Hours of work.

And it's just my lifestyle. My lifestyle is waking up in the morning and recording music.

TUV: You talk about being a different voice in this thing, and I agree. You'll make an album about *Dragonball Z*, or *One Piece*, you'll do these concepts, and if we take the content alone – I think one would have an impression of you – they would expect you – to be of a particular 'brand' of emcee. But you're not that. I don't think the term 'nerdcore' is ever appropriate, but I think a lot of cats would expect a particular sound or aesthetic to be paired with this content. But you're shit is hard. It's almost street rap. It is street rap at times. But it has that underlining current. I don't see others doing this. You occupy a unique lane. It's like the best of both worlds… and then just as a technician? You're fucking dope! [Laughs] It's a beautiful blend, I can't get enough… seriously. It's good.

NDL: I appreciate that. Cause look, that street element is all me man. Growing in Washington DC, I was born in Paris France… Then lived in Brooklyn. It's all urban life. I've only lived in big cities. When I meet a lot of my rap peers, it feels like a lot of us like what some would consider nerdy. Cats will listen to anime, watch different things, but it just often doesn't translate into music. For me, I allow it to translate into music. I remember listening to **Method Man** on *P.L.O. Style* where he says, "I'm the true fist of the North Star." So I'm like, "I know he watches anime…" And I was younger then, but I was already watching Japanese stuff for example, so it highly influenced me as a kid because I was getting tapes from overseas and I was living in that universe where Is tarted to understand that culture. For me, hip-hop is a great conduit for all of these ideas and that aesthetic. That Shonen Anime aesthetic. It inspired me as a kid because Shonen Anime is like anime mostly made for boys. Stereotypically. Everybody watches it now, but… It's like a young kid, that's lost in the world, that's probably a little bit weak, that's realizing that the world is full of monsters and they get bigger and bigger and you gotta train to conquer your demons – your monsters – and then you go through the whole circle, the hero journey. That's kind of like me in hip-hop. I'm just this kid who's loving hip-hop naively. I love this culture. Like, "let me do it!" and the more you get into it, the more you're like, "wow, I wasn't ready for what this is. The business and the machine of what this is. I was there, sitting at... I was invited for meetings at **Universal**, at **Sony**, talking about doing this or that, and it just never fanning out. And me, just being like, "I love this. I've never did this so that I can be under contract for a company, I did this so that I could make great music." And now with technology, you're able to do that at your own level. I'm like, "why not?"

So me merging all this together. And just sounding how I sound everyday. I remember one time, I don't really sit out and listen to everything people say about me, cause sometimes things come up, you'll read a comment or something... Somebody was criticizing one of my albums, he's like, "I don't like Napoleon Da Legend because he has so many 'life-affirming lines.' Like what? I'm supposed to be death affirming? Like, "yo!" To me, it's so backwards. We lived in the urban areas, doing what we did, going from job to job to survive, hustling, going through little jobs... We already got a **Mobb Deep**, we already got these really dark apocalyptic vibe from rappers. I just want a bigger spectrum. I just want to open it up. There's some songs where I'm going to talk shit and I'mma be negative. And I'mma show you that evil personality that I got naturally. That I always had, since I was playing basketball back in the days. And everything else that I did. But also, there's times where... yo man, I can't drown myself into a depression of always being negative. Always around snakes, or people that I don't enjoy, or people that I got to calculate and think. I want to think positively. Why not add all that into my rhymes? I'm trying to give you the gammit of what my mindstate is, and not just a sliver of it.

And I'm not under pressure to sell product. Some rappers gotta sell you that product because they know, that's the crack. That's what

people want... People get high off that. "You love to hear the story how the thugs live in worry." **Nas** said it. That story sells. And that story has been sold, repackaged, remixed, a million different times. I'm like, "what can I do to where, I know that story, but I also know this other story. Let me tell something else, cause I think there's room for that." I think there's space for me to do what I am.

TUV: I've had a thought over the years, that rap music is one of the few art forms that exist – perhaps literature as well, where any knowledge can assist in you becoming better at the art. Rap is a puzzle, and knowledge are the pieces you have at your disposal. [It allows reading a book, or a comic, or watching a video, or having a conversation with a friend, it allows these activities to be akin to opening up a pack of trading cards. Tools you gather to assist in your game.] I think that's a powerful aspect of hip-hop. It's what makes the creativity so endless. 90% of rap is people coming up with unique ways to say that 'I'm better than you.' The fact that that can even happen, is fascinating. But you're right. A lot of cats don't seize that opportunity. You seem to be a person who understands that value and embraces the life that can come with that. When knowledge and experience become skillsets, it makes you wanna experience more life.

NDL: I love that about it. If you listen to the project I did with **Clypto**, *Maison de Medici,* the reason I called it *Maison de Medici,* is that's the rich family that funded a lot of the art during the renaissance. Leonardo Di Vinci, Michael Angelo, for a few months I just got obsessed with the renaissance. The Italian Renaissaince, then the Northern Renaissance... and the beats he was sending me. .. I don't know why some producers send me different beats. I think I'm a little bit more open, I think probably a lot of beats they leave, a lot of rappers are like, "nah, give me

that hard shit." And some of the beats [Clypto] was giving me was making me feel like I was sitting in the Garden of Eden. If you listen to the song *Baritone Paradox* for example, all of that was just a whole bunch of references to Renaissance art. And putting it into context. The same thing for painting, your paint can be the same as everybody else, as we hear the same words, have the same rap references, I could channel my inner Wu, my inner **50 Cent,** my inner Mobb Deep, etc. But let me add other things to the pallet. That's what I like to have; an extremely diverse - extremely exotic - pallet. I'mma give you totally different imagery and transport you somewhere else for the two or three minutes of the song.

TUV: I think that life should service the art, and not the other way around. Enjoy the lifetime, do things, experience things, have fun, and allow the art to be a product of that. But not the other way around. A lot of cats I think have that mixed up.

NDL: You know one thing that the late, great, **Sean Price,** whom to me was like a mentor... we've collaborated, he's given advice, and I think he was giving an interview, I forget which one, and he said, "don't let hip-hop ruin your life." That stuck with me a lot. A lot of rappers won't say that, but I get what he means. There's stuff that will ruin your life in hip-hop. If you're into always being so reckless, beefing, drugs, this that and the third, it's like if you put your mind only to the space, ten years from now, your life won't be good. For me, I'm just taking my experiences. I come from outside of hip-hop in a way. I was born somewhere else and I grew up in the DC / Maryland area. It's not really like a hip-hop city back then. There was hip-hop, but there was other things going on... And then going to New York where I really started to pursue a career? You meet your rap heroes and being naive, you think you're going to get the person you hear on the record. Like, "I thought this person was going to like punch me in the face when I met him!" I'm being extra, I didn't think that... but I was being a little bit naive as a fan. But they're like regular people. They've had jobs, they've got fired, they're just like me... but I never hear them talk about that.

I think it would bring so much to the culture. Like, we live for this hip-hop. Hip-Hop makes us feel good. We listen to it because we need too. But why were you nice for like three years of your career then we never heard from you again, twenty years later? What happened in those years? A lot of people don't explain stuff like that. That's why I like to take you through my experiences, like, there's times where I didn't think I could pay the rent. There's times I've had minimum wage jobs... I like to talk about it because a lot of rappers will only talk about the car chase where they were getting shots fired at them and what not. Which is fine, it's super interesting, it's like an action movie... but sometimes it's like, "yo, bring is through the real emotional drama of life." I'm really more about the cinematic emotional drama that life brings you. With the highs, and the lows.

TUV: Fair enough. I don't want to keep you too much longer here, but I did want to ask before you go - you mentioned a triple-album before the end of the year, but even before that - I know you put out a lot of music, what can we expect from NDL in the coming months?

NDL: Yeah, what's coming next... Next month you can expect, kind of in the same theme of inspiration as D-Styles, I have an album coming out produced by **J Scienide** called *Goats vs. Sheep*.

TUV: Doope! And J-Scienide on the beats too? I think of J-Scienide still as an emcee. So that's really cool to see.

NDL: Yeah, well J-Scienide is a dope ass producer and it's the first time that he produced for a rapper like that. It was his idea. We met in DC through a mutual friend and he was like, "i wanna produce an album for you." He raps on there too, so you'll hear his bars, but it's my album. It's crazy because within the last three months, both J-Scienide and myself have had an album produced by **Giallo Point** in the UK. We both got a D-Styles album. And now we have a collaboration album coming out, which is pretty in-

teresting. Then I got a second album with Clypto coming out, and you'll see some dope collabs on that too. Cause I love working with Clypto, on a human level too, he's really a good dude. And he has a good ear for loops, he's a loop-master.

Then I got a triple album produced by myself. It's what I want to end the year off with. Cause I don't know if I'll go on a hiatus, cause I still probably have projects finished out there that I can't think about, but I put a lot into that. I wanted to really speak on my life in a real cinematic manner. It's like an emotional opera album. AlbumS. They can be listened to all at once, but I realize you can't give people 40 joints, so I chopped them up into three acts. They're stand alone, but they're all linked. So I look forward to being able to drop that too.

TUV: Man, I'm excited for anything and everything you put out. Like I've said, you're one of my favourite emcees and it's always a pleasure to get hit with new NDL material.

AZizz

TUV: Let's start with Slang Doe Records. Obviously, Slang Ton, RIP, passed away in 1999. After that event, you end up creating Slang Doe Records. Are you able to tell that story? Of how Slang Doe Records came to be?

Absolutely. **Slang Doe Records**... Okay, so in the early 90s, I want to say 94-95, I had a friend that was Brazilian, his name was **Skills** [**Skilarela**, or **BSkills**], he was Brazilian. So, we'd be in Jersey... we were broke, homeless, walking the streets, and he was pretty cool. He was a hustler. So, he used to be like, "yo! get the train! come to Philly and chill with us!" I'm like, "mannn, how much is the train?" But somehow, I'd get the bread and I'd get there, and we'd be in Philly. When we get to Broad and Erie Ave, we'd get out and Skills would pull up, like, "what you trying to do? You just need to smoke." But he would always have lick-shots. I'm not sure if you know what a lick-shot is, but a lick-shot is promethazine with a Percocet in the bottle. Back then, they called it 'snot' because it looked yellow like snot. They used to sell it on J Street in Philly. So boom, we drink this, start smoking... I didn't know what it was when I first tried it. Tried it, I woke up at 3:00am in the morning, and we got there at like 12:00pm. But we woke up at 3:00am in the morning. Me, **100Geezs**, **Ribs [Ribsdoe]**, **Satu**, Slang [Slang-Ton], Bskills, Doe and a couple of other people. We all jumped into the pool at Hunting Park in Philadelphia. That was like some magical ceremonial stuff that was spiritual or something, cause after that, Doe, [which] was BSkills right-hand man, and Skills friend was Ribs. And Ribs and Doe were cousins. So after that we all became hella cool. So we would all go to Philly with those guys. One weekend, we got a phone call, and Doe had

got killed. So Doe died. Slang died. Before Slang died, we had started the project, *All Natural*.

We had already had a project before Slang died; *All Natural*. It ended up being the very first Outsidaz album. It just wasn't spearheaded by [**Pace** and **Zee**]. If you listen to *All Natural*, I produced the whole EP. It featured Slang, **Luen-1**, Pace.. it featured everybody. If I'm not mistaken, there's probably only one person who didn't make it, and [that was **Eminem**]. And now that Slang had passed, we had the songs and boom, we dropped the album. We were happy.

And then [the] *Night Life EP* comes out. I mean, they got an opportunity to do the album with a major label. We were all independent at the time with the 'Slang Doe' name. They didn't want to come rock with Slang Doe and rock with us. I wasn't a big fan of signing my life away, never was. So, boom. We just did a label in memory of our brothers, and we just had songs already recorded and put it all out on *All Natural*. So boom. That's the first **Outsidaz** al-

lbum. And it came out on Slang Doe Records. I was the producer, artist, owner. Skills was the CEO and Ribs was the CO. But we all co-owned the label and we was all like one unit.

So it was me, Ribs and Skills who started Slang Doe Records, and put out All Natural, the very first Outsidaz album.

TUV: Now when you say the 'very first Outsidaz album,' on Discogs, it shows the record comes out in 2000. That's a couple years after both Zee's *Musical Meltdown*, and The *Pacewon Effect*, but both of those have label issues and don't get proper releases. Can you clarify what you mean here.

All Natural was recorded while Slang was alive. So it was all recorded earlier. Late 95, early 96' we started recording *All Natural*. But we had already had the product done long before 2000. I'll say this. It only came out in 2000 because we didn't have the knowledge of how to do that. As far as the way it looks? It looks like it came out after, but it's because we were selling hard copies - way before. We had the product done, but it didn't get to the people, it didn't [get] publish until later.

So the album was done. Everybody was on it, then we got the opportunity to do the EP [*Nightlife*] in 97', around the same time. Those songs were all getting recorded and [there

was] jealousy that we had the product. Then we started working on the Outsidaz EP. So in the system, and I could be wrong, but the way that I remember it, I was already at **Perfect Pair Studio** working on these songs way before the Outsidaz project.

TUV: Gotcha. So as you said, for All Natural, all the members of the Outz are on it. When this is being recorded, was it all recorded with the pretence that these joints were going to be for an Az Izz solo album? Or was any of it to go on a group effort?

Yeah, it was my compilation album. It was my solo album but I turned it into a compilation album because the singles that were off of there were all solo songs. Like, *Ya'll Can't Mess With the Az*, that was a solo song... *Probly You*, was a solo song on there... I had *Suicide* with DU. So there's some records on there... but all of that stuff was solely mines because I was that guy, you know what I mean?

<table>
<tr><td>14.</td><td>

The Miseducation Of Lauryn Hill [++]

</td></tr>
</table>

My world it moves so fast today / The past it seems so far away / And I squeeze it so tight, I can't breathe / And every time I try to be / What someone has thought of me / So caught up, I wasn't able to achieve / But deep in my heart the answer it was in me / And I made up my mind to find my own destiny / I look at my environment / And wonder where the fire went / What happened to everything we used to be / I hear so many cry for help / Searching outside of themselves / Now I know His strength is within me / And deep in my heart the answer it was in me / And I made up my mind to find my own destiny / And deep in my heart the answer it was in me / And I made up my mind to find my own destiny

Vocals: Lauryn Hill • Fender Rhodes & Organ: Loris Holland • Piano: Joe Wilson • Strings: Indigo Quartet • Recorded by Tony Prendatt • Engineered by Comissioner Gordon and Tony Prendatt • Mixed by Comissioner Gordon • Assisted by Storm Jefferson • Recorded and Mixed at Chung King Studios, NYC • © 1998 Sony/ATV Tunes LLC/Obverse Creation Music/Jermaine Music (ASCAP)/All rights for Sony/ATV Tunes LLC and Obverse Creation Music administered by Sony/ ATV Music Publishing, 8 Music Square West, Nashville. All Rights Reserved. Used by Permission.

TUV: Around that time, if you go back and read old interviews, you see the Outsidaz promoting Outhouse Records and then later obviously we get the material on Ruffhouse. Why feel the need to create a splinter label with Slang Doe? Why not consolidate it all under one umbrella?

Skills was an honorary member of the Outsidaz, you know what I mean? Cause of how he moved, and what he did for us, how he helped us out in the hardest time of our lives. Dude used to really let us come stay at his house when we had no place to go in Jersey and we got tired of walking around. So he became an honorary member. If you look at the Slang Doe stuff, it's so close to that *Nightlife EP*, we were working on that, first. And once that was already out, and everybody messed with it, I didn't have a chance to keep going because now I'm stuck in a contract. This is where the Outhouse comes in. Let me clear the Outhouse thing up.

Outsidaz first signed to **Columbia Records** / I think **Ruff Nation**. We were directly under Columbia because **Chris Schwartz** had his situation with Columbia. For some reason, Chris Schwartz wanted to leave Columbia. So he left Columbia, and **Warner Brothers** gave him like a 40 million dollar deal, or whatever the amount was, I don't remember clearly, so he took that deal and he brought The Outsidaz to his label independently. What they didn't do with us, is they didn't sign the Outsidaz directly to Warner Brothers, or **RuffLife Records**, or Ruff Nation Records. Or **Ruffhouse Records**. They signed The Outsidaz to Outworld Productions. Right?

So Zee, Pace, [Rah] Digga are the owners of **Outworld Productions**. I was only in the country for about 5 years, so I had no clue how the business worked. So I ended up signing as a producer to Outworld Records. Everything I produced, I was going to get 50% of, and that's what I did.

Perfect Pair Records was ran by Ken Johnston. It was previously ran under the name, 'Eastern Artists Recording Studios.' Located in East Orange, New Jersey. Discogs has a series of albums recorded at the studio - most notably being Lauryn Hill's *Miseducation*. I've tried to verify this claim, but cannot. The liner notes show it was recorded at Chung King Studios. This is a minor detail, but I'd love to get this cleared up. Lots of Jersey artists recorded at Perfect Pair. Perhaps the dopest cut that I've seen is Posneg's *No Death* 12" in 1997. [Posneg is a group from the South Bronx]

So when The Outsidaz got the budget money, Zee, Pace and Digga only gave each Outsida $2,000.00 to sign to Outworld Productions - which was signed to Ruff Life Records. Which was an independent record company that Chris Schwartz, who owned RuffHouse, changed from RuffHouse to RuffNation. And that's how we started.

So now the major is Warner Brothers, the subsidiary is RuffNation Records, but the mom and pop company? Is RuffLife Records. And that's who they signed The Outsidaz too. They never gave us a major deal bro. They gave the money to Zee, Pace and Digga and they shitted on The Outsidaz.

That's why the project wasn't as good as it should have been, as far as the *Bricks* album. So that's the whole pretence of Outworld, RuffLife, RuffNation, RuffHouse... So they never signed directly to the majors. That's why we never had the budget like the **Fugees**, and we didn't do those videos...

TUV: Going through the old SlangDoe and Outsidaz websites, there was a variant called Slang-a-Ton Records, which was apparently supposed to drop, what I can only imagine is a BSkills solo album called, 'Deported Skilarela Relaskila to Brazil' Can you tell me anything about Slang-a-Ton and this BSkills album? Cause I don't think it ever came out, did it?

Yeah, yeah, it never came out. That's Skills just being Skills. Skills loved hip-hop and he got deported from the US and so he went back to Brazil. When he got back there he was just trying to get an album together with some Brazilian people. But I don't think it panned out. But Slang-A-Ton Records? And all of that stuff? That was just a name he thought of. Slang-Doe Records is actually an official name that me, him and Ribs were owners of. And we ran like young entrepreneurs. Like I said, I was always independent, I never understood why I have to give somebody my money when we didn't need no marketing. We was already up. You know what I mean? So that's how it went man. So Skilarela and Slang Doe? That's my right hand man, my best friend. Know what I mean? And he's always been our corner in a positive light. So Skills, if you see this? Respect, love and appreciate everything brother. He should be over here coming back soon too.

TUV: I'm so happy I have you on the line here to be able to answer of some of these questions. This is great. Related to the same era, the group 'The Dopeliss.' It was Slang-Ton and Luen-1 from what I can gather. Pace talked about it in a 1998 interview with Werner. Can you share any details on The Dopeliss? What did they do?

Absolutely! Absolutely. So, I'll make this easy for you... So the Outsidaz is a bunch of different crews. Rap crews, that were already existing that came together. So in the beginning, Pace and Zee and **DU** were solo acts. I think they had a producer, DU had his rap partner and Pace's group was called **Prepared Never Scared**, and DU's group was called **The Teammates**. Zee and his brother **Yah Yah** had **No Brains Class**. No Brains Class had a deal with some company, I forgot... but they were the first ones with a record deal. Zee and his brother. Slang and Luen, they were **Dopeliss**.

In the recesses of Newark, New Jersey—amid a ghetto so desolate it would make East St. Louis blush—lies the Outhouse, the headquarters for Brick City supergroup The Outsidaz. As befits their standing as Jersey underground royalty, their three-story tenement—a renovated crack shack—is a monument to urban hardship: Red paint flakes from the walls. A piece of cardboard with the address scrawled on it dangles from the front door. Inside, crooked nails jut from walls; the doors lack knobs. And what seems like a year's worth of Dutch Master innards covers the floor. ✳ Scarred and neglected, yet somehow still standing, the Outhouse also symbolizes the group that calls it home. Cobbled together from two rival graffiti crews, The Outsidaz have toiled for six years in the Jersey shadows. Though rappers Pace-Won and Young-Zee are the heart and soul of the ever-growing massive, The Outz also include Jersey representatives Axe; Rah Digga (who has a daughter with Zee); Slang Ton (winner of last month's Blaze Battle); Az-Izz; D.U.; Zee's older brother, Yah-Yah; Denzy; DJ Mohamed; and Luen 1. Detroit MCs Eminem—yes, Eminem—and Bizarre Kid are also down. ✳ The group saw its first exposure in 1996, when Zee, Digga and Pace appeared on the Fugees' hit "Cowboys." But problems arose. Critics panned Zee's debut, *Musical Meltdown*, before its release, prompting Perspective/A&M Records to stop promoting it. Around the same time, The Outsidaz's producer Skillz was sentenced to life in prison for murder. Although group members have turned up on other records—Zee with Redman and Gov-Mattic on "Cloze Ya Doorz"; Digga with Busta Rhymes on the Flipmode Squad album—The Outsidaz have yet to receive their props. ✳ That could change soon. The Outsidaz recently inked a deal with Ruffhouse/Columbia, following the success of their independent single "Rain Or Shine." Their album, tentatively titled *Outz World '99*, is slated for release in August. Rah Digga, Eminem, Pace-Won and Young-Zee have solo deals. Pace's debut album, *The Pace-Won Effect*, is due this summer; Zee's and Digga's, later this year. ✳ But as evidenced by the shanty they call home, The Outz don't live like stars; their time in the Bricks is often spent peddling herbals, ingesting a pharmacopoeia of cheap drugs and rhyming—always rhyming. "The Bricks is like hell wrapped up in a sesame-seed bun," says Young-Zee. Lyrically, The Outsidaz's lighthearted—if lawless—demeanor lands them somewhere between the street-corner hustling of N.W.A and the dusted hallucinations of the Pharcyde. ✳ Because of the group's size, each MC must battle his or her way onto songs: "There are 12 of us, and we can't have 12 people on one song. So if you're not fresh, then you're just not gonna be on any songs." They take the challenge so seriously that they often refuse to reveal their verses to each other until the first vocal take. But despite its competitiveness, the collective stays tight. "We love each other like brothers," says Zee. "So even if we don't ever make it in this rap   , we still gonna be just a fun-ass clique!" ◌

I met Slang and Luen... See Luen's brother used to be in a rap group. I used to be like his producer / DJ at first, who was helping at first, but then I started rapping for them. I had done one song with them, performing at this club **Little Shields.** After we had performed the song at Little Shields, and when I did my verse, and automatically people turned and looked at me. That's how I knew I had something. But Luen's brother, he's the one who introduced me to Slang and Luen. And also, I went to school with Luen's cousin -   **K-Mill** -AKA **Get's Dope**. You can just say, 'Get's Dope.' So Get's Dope was always trying to get me to meet The Outsidaz when I was in high school, but I was brand new in the country, listening to my mom's religiously, so I just went to school and came home. And went to my cousins crib. I ain't fuck with nobody in America. I stayed away.

But when I graduated, I was like, "yeah, I'll go meet these guys." So Slang and Luen showed up to my door one day and they were homeless. This was like 96. I'll never forget it. They had icicles on their face so I let them in my house and they started rapping! And I'm blown away. Like, "these mothafuckas are fresh as hell!" I ain't never heard nobody rap like this. My mom's was like, you know... "you can't have your friends stay here..." I was like, "mom, I'm leaving! And when I come back, I'mma be fresh like these guys." And I started walking the streets with Slang and Luen and became Dopeliss. So Dopeliss was Luen-1, Slang-Ton and **DJ Third Rail,** before I became the fourth member. So I was apart of Dopeliss before the Outz.

Slang and Lou were kind of schooling me in how to be Dopeliss. Which was like, using a lot of syllables in one bar. Before, all those other guys, they had the Dr. Seuss raps. The story telling, **Slick Rick** type raps, and it was kind of boring. It got boring. Slang just came out of nowhere with this style. So Dopeliss was me, Slang, Luen, and Third Rail.

I never wanted to meet [The Outsidaz]. I never cared. But one day Slang convinced me to go around them. And when I went around them, I seen the energy. I'm an only child so I didn't have no brothers, and it was cool to be around some dudes.

It took me like a year to get fresh but I spent like three months in jail. Came home, started writing, and started really taking it seriously. So, Slang and Luen was like, "you gotta kick it with us more." Just them being around me, and showing me exactly just what 'fresh' is. I was able to learn on my own. Like nobody ever told me, like, "you should write down all your rhyming words first", or "say this…" Know what I mean? Nobody ever gave me no pointers, I learned it on my own. So I became Dopeliss. And then Slang, when I was good enough, Slang told me I could rap now. And then I started rapping, and boom. [I] did it with a passion, and the rest is history. Cause I started kicking up, battling everybody from East Orange, New Jersey, downtown, north of the Arcade…

And back then, me, Slang and Luen, we hung on Eppirt Street a lot. Cause DJ Third Rail, who was Dopeliss's DJ, he used to run on Eppirt Street on East Orange a lot. And Eppirt Street had a lot of talent. Me and DJ Third Rail was dope. **DJ Dark Man** was dope. And **DJ Mud**, who was Zee and Yah's first DJ - No Brains Class' DJ - he was there as well, but we all used to be on Eppirt Street. The first person who took a liking to me when I got to the country, was the person who brought me on Eppirt Street, and his name was **Perez**. And Perez was the one the one that really brought me outside around the rap crew.

Before that I was DJing. The minute I got to the country I was DJing. Basement parties with my cousin after like two years, you know what I mean? So we used to try to have fun and we didn't have nowhere to go, but my aunt had a pretty big basement. My uncle had a pretty big basement, both of them. And we would just throw parties, don't charge nobody, and just have a good time with the people that we went to school with. We used to play basketball in the back yard. One day, we started charging and somebody brought a gun in and that was the end of it. But yeah man, we used to have fun back then. You know what I mean?

TUV: Dopeliss. Did you guys ever put anything out as Dopeliss?

Dopeliss? Slang and Luen got two songs that they did, like in the mix of becoming Dopeliss, but by the time they got fresh - the Outsidaz thing took off. But Dopeliss only got a couple songs. I got them somewhere online, but they never got a full project. There was just no where to record back in those days. Like you had to have money and a job, and like I said, me, Slang and Luen were like parked in the streets on some nomad stuff. But when we did get the opportunity to go to different studios, we would go lay a verse or something like that, but I don't remember them having a full project, no.

TUV: I love the fact that you ended up mentioning DJ Third Rail. I had that name written down and wanted to ask you about him. I just came off of doing a deep dive into a San Diego rap collective called Masters of the Universe from the 90s. And they had a DJ Third Rail. And I think there's a cat in Chicago with the name as well. But your Third Rail… So he's Dopeliss's DJ, can you provide more insight into this cat? Did he ever put anything out? Did he go on to do his thing after the Outz?

DJ Third Rail, he ended up DJing, but he started producing. And I think he did some

Sixteen MCs put the "ill" in Illadelph at the Blaze MC Battle

CASHMERE

AZ-IZ

McCLOUD

INTRO BY CHARISSE NIKOLE. BRACKETS BY HYUN KIM. ASSISTS BY TONE BOOTS, NOAH CALLAHAH-BEVER, ZHOU DAO-YI, STEFANIE DOUGLAS AND RICH MEDINA AT BOBBITO'S FOOTWORK ILLADELPH

All hell broke loose at Philadelphia's Evolution nightclub when the Blaze Battle tour touched down. The crowd and contestants wasted little time turning the event from cipher to circus. The ringmasters were the infamous Mobb Deep, and Havoc and Prodigy's thugged-out antics made for one rah-rah spectacle. From the hurling of trash at wack contestants to the Mobb's unapologetic favoritism to the ousting of unskilled MCs by the dumns — Philly was backdrop to the unruliest battle to date.

A few younger contestants were knocked out even before the first punch line was thrown. After barely skimming past bouncers reviewing IDs like IRS auditors, 19-year-old MCs I.B. Dasderdly and Sakrifice were removed from the club for drinking. "They're throwing me out because they're scared of the truth," Sak said outside while fighting back tears. "I didn't know it would be that harsh," I.B. groaned after failed attempts to polly his way back inside. While I.B. and Sak chilled (more like froze) in the parking lot, substitutes Destro and Shawn Lav got put on.

The telltale sign the night was going awry came during the very first battle. Not satisfied with verses exchanged by Valentine and El Juba, an unknown PKA surfaced onstage to the crowd's utter confusion, spilling incomprehensible lines before Mobb and meter man Tone Boots silenced him. Despite distractions, the battle waged on. The night ultimately belonged to Slang Ton, whose rhymes and a cappella performance beat North Carolina's Jon NOTTY in the finals. Slang got a big boost from his 20-deep Outsidaz crew, which was strategically scattered throughout the venue. "I was destined to win this ___," exclaimed Slang before taking the stage with his crew for a post-battle performance and celebration. After past battle losses by Outsidaz Young-Zee and Pace-Won, the crown finally ended up in "the Outhouse."

Winners & Losers: Numbers are *Blaze* sound-meter scores, in decibels. "nada" is the meter reading when audience response was less than 100 dbs.

ROUND ONE

El Juba [113] defeats Valentine [109] Before Valentine could respond to El Juba's attack — "I make you put down your mic and leave like Ginger Spice" — an unknown MC snatched the mic and rattled off a few lines, confusing the crowd.

Jon NOTTY [114] def. Az-Iz [104] Az-Iz tried to win over the booing crowd with tired punch lines like "I kick ___ like Pele." Then, finally fed up, he addressed his audience, "All you niggas booin'/ Y'all can get a dick lick."

Bugz [112] def. Pred [107] In one of the less eventful battles, Bugz started making physical threats against Pred, who was jeered 20 seconds into his verse.

Invincible [113] def. Sub-Conscious [110] An otherwise lethargic Havoc grew eager for this match when Invincible, resembling Raggedy Ann, stepped up. Sub-Conscious kicked abstract freestyles. Invincible put the dread away with "Bob Marley?/ You're just a carbon copy."

Destro [108] def. K.A.O. [nada] After only 30 seconds, K.A.O. becomes the first MC in Blaze Battle history to be ushered offstage by a host. During the first 29, the crowd pelted him with debris. Havoc declared a "double lose" after both MCs got low responses.

Slang Ton [113] def. McCloud a.k.a. Golden Eye [nada] Slang Ton easily tossed McCloud to the side with his clear delivery and arrogance: "You bastard/ You're full of ___ like a faggot's mattress." Buckling under pressure, McCloud was left fumbling his words and, eventually, chuckling to himself in resignation.

Too Maa [107] def. Cashmere the PROfessional [102] Cashmere kept referring to shorty's pre-written verses and got a good response with a shot at Too Maa's oversized gear: "After I'm done/ I want my pants back." But Too Maa, a 15-year-old prodigy, prevailed even after being forced to kick his rapid flow twice when the timer didn't start.

Priest Da Named [109] def. Shawn Lav [nada] As Shawn Lav stepped onto the stage, a heckler greeted him by hurling a Heineken bottle. Priest sealed his victory with a jab at the rappin' George Michael lookalike, "Now who's it gonna be?/ Me/ Or maybe this 90210 extra."

ROUND TWO

Jon NOTTY [115] def. El Juba [Lo] Jon Notty kicked what was arguably the best opening line of the night: "I'm a Wildcat like Tubby/ Down in Kentucky/ If your chicken ain't ugly/ I'ma book her like Chuckii." El Juba mustered a weak response: "Yo, you/ You're a bum/ You were raised on crumbs."

Invincible [108] def. Bugz [102] In one of the more entertaining battles, Invincible swung first: "Oh, your name's Bugz?/ I hit you with a flyswatter." Even while receiving boos from the crowd, Bugz managed to sneak in one good line: "You're dirt like potted soil/ Plus your image's finished/ You hippie Olive Oyl."

Slang Ton [113] def. Destro [102] Destro desperately threatened to rip Slang's dreads and his crew, the Outsidaz. Slang fired back a cappella: "You're stupid like lickin' cuts/ On AIDS patients' lips and butts."

Too Maa [112] def. Priest Da Named [109] Both MCs went for the jugular. Priest: "You got African beads, come on you don't love me/ Damn, you should be at home watching Teletubbies." Too Maa: "Once this ___ nigga steps inside my death quarter/ I'll turn Priest into a born-again-Christian."

ROUND THREE

Jon NOTTY [112] def. Invincible [106] NOTTY got racial, urging the crowd to "look at this white girl/ She needs to try out for the Spice Girls." Then he called her a "nigger" and suggested she had Klan ties. But Invincible lynched herself: "You say I'm down with the KKK/ Alright alright OK/ You get tarred and feathered." Needless to say, the mostly black audience booed her ass.

Slang Ton [115] def. Too Maa [113] The crowd got hyped by the instrumental to Cool Breeze's "Watch for the Hook," but booed when Slang eschewed the beat. He rocked a cappella briefly, then with 20 seconds remaining, called for music. Too Maa's irrelicate rhymes flew over most people's heads. Slang closed with a dis: "You're see-through like Scotch tape/ You get took out like hot dates."

THE FINAL

JON NOTTY [LEFT] VS. SLANG TON

ROUND FOUR

Slang Ton [115] def. Jon NOTTY [109] Jon NOTTY had the crowd's support early on, but stammered his second time around with "aho," "ums" and "yeahs." Seizing the opportunity, Slang again went a cappella, warning NOTTY: "If I get a hold of your wack-ass demo/ It's gettin' dubbed over." Game over.

Slang Ton
WINNER OF THE BLAZE MC BATTLE, February 24, 1999, Philadelphia

beats for... for an artist... I think he helped **El Da Sensei** with some beats from **The Artifacts**, he did some beats for someone, but I can't remember the name. But he started producing stuff. Production credits. But he never put out a DJ project out, nah. Because Third Rail, wasn't like a blend DJ, he was more like a skill DJ, like the **Roc Raida's** and stuff. That's who they idolized. They idolized Roc Raida and those guys.

TUV: I wanted to ask you about the 1999 Blaze Emcee Battle in Philadelphia. I was reading an article and it seems as though Slang-Ton actually won that shit, but you were there, there's a photo of you. Do you remember this Blaze Battle?

I remember it well brother. It was two battles that happened that day. The first battle was me and the guy who was from Philadelphia who had my name Az Izz. So I'm in the club, and this guy walks up to me and says "yo! this dude says his name is Az Izz!" I said, "man, fuck outta here." Like, we gotta battle. So me and him battled, I took him out, won my name. Then it's Slang's time, and Slang's on stage, and this is the **Blaze Battle**, and this is the moment that me, Slang and Luen had been waiting on.

But anyway, fast forward back to the Slang shit and the 99 Blaze Battle... So boom. If you know anything about the Blaze Battles in the 90s, they were two opponents. It was you. It was artist in front of you. And then the crowd. The crowd was the one's who chose who won the battle. Slang just went up there and started going crazy. So like I said, Philly is my second home. We was deep! Philly dudes was there. Jersey dudes was there, it was deep! So as Slang was rapping, every bar we knew it, so we would react! Banging on the thing! Glass bottles! Just loudness... So he ended up taking the battle.

So now, he won the Blaze Battle. And back then, when you won the battle, you either went straight to **Def Jam** or somewhere else... you got signed. Nobody ever offered anything to him to go and shop his product. It was just this sinister-hate or jealousy that was always there... They never wanted him to be like the leader and best of the group. So Slang won, Slang came home... and he's thinking he's going to be signed to Def Jam. Somebody's going to give him a deal that he just won. They did nothing. So what me and Slang did was, we did side deals. Cause we was already signed to RuffLife, but what me and Slang did, we got with **Michael Houston** and we got with a young lady called **Egypt**,

, **U'Seff Majjid**... His rap name was **Majjid**. We got with **Supreme C**... So it was me, Slang, Supreme C, Egypt, U'Seff Majjid and Omega. And we formed this group called The Anonymous Clik. **Newark Anonymous Clik.**

When we formed the group, we ended up signing to **Bobby Brown** and **Whitney Houston**. But we was also signed to RuffNation, and you couldn't have two record deals with two different groups back then. So the second group, Slang didn't care, he didn't hide his face, but I hid my face... So we did some records, **Funk Master Flex** I heard was playing the record... A week after we left before we went to go on tour with The Outsidaz, Flex was dropping bombs on our records!

So Slang and I started being a little rebellious. You know what I mean? I'm like, "I'm producing hella records. I'm rapping fresh. I'm setting all these songs off, I'm the hottest nigga in the Outsidaz! How the fuck is noone trying to sign me to a solo deal. And then we just figured, let's go get our own shit! When we did that, that's when we started understanding the business. The contracts started coming to us while we were out on tour. They were trying to get us to sign to Outworld Productions again, and this is after we dropped the EP. We have a fanbase... we got Eminem signed... Giving him the street credibility and just coming around us, putting him on stage to open up for us. Know what I mean? Sharing his EP with our audience... Know what I mean? Dude's in our community... Just showing him hell of love. And that's where we were like, "we were willing to do anything for Em and these guys wasn't really willing to do nothing for us. And we were already in a position before he got here. So that shit was like sad to us, and we just got tired with the back and forth. Luen had started losing his... mind, you know? He started being a little mentally ill. So he wasn't rapping the same anymore. A lot of the songs that Luen was on, you'd have

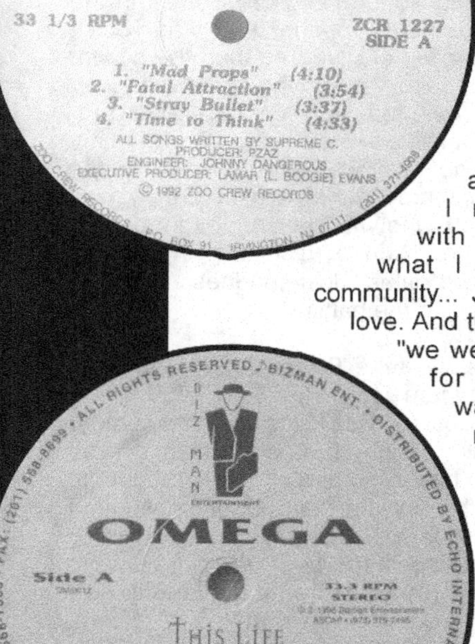

to go to **Musical Meltdown** to hear Luen rap. You wasn't hearing him on the Outsidaz project cause he wasn't making sense. The last project that Luen rapped on was *All Natural*. You know what I mean?

TUV: There's a lot there to go through. I know we're at the 40 minute mark here, but I do have a few more questions if you have some time.

Yeah, go ahead! Shoot!

TUV: I wanted to ask you about The Outhouse. It's become this legendary and iconic spot in underground rap lore. Can you paint the picture of what it was like at the Outhouse?

The Outhouse was a trap house / a rap house. Everybody in the Outhouse sold weed to pay their bills. That was the first or second floor. On the third floor is where the raps went. So you had competition through the whooooole house. The Outhouse would set them to do a song. It was simple man. Even though we were in competition, you made certain people keep their head turned... Like even with me. When Em came around, I think somebody did the beat for *Macosa*, the beat was playing... we're writing our rhymes and when it's time to spit, it's like, "what the hell are you going to say?" and nobody would say shit. And I just put the mic on him and motherfucka started rapping on the mic, and the person who's verses were best, we just kept those verses... If you're verse wasn't good, we took it off. But usually back then, you have a one-off track, or two tracks to rap on. Which was one for your adlibs and one for your verse. So you really ain't have no time to go back and re-do the shit. It was like one take or nothing - you're off

the song. So when Em came on the *Macosa* joint, and stepped right up and did his thing. And we kept him on the song. He wasn't even signed or nothing. That's another thing that I got to mention. They didn't see the most awesomeness bag in front of their face. Em came to Jersey to sign as an Outsida. His whole shit was that he wanted to be an Outsida. He wanted to sign with us, he wanted to be down. You know what I'm saying? But they didn't sign him. They didn't even sign him to the production company. The way that we would be responsible to make some beats for him. It was like a beautiful competitive room of dope ass emcees. At that time, believe it or not, we supported each other. We loved each other. Until the money came. When the people who never had money got money, it changed them and it destroyed our little ambience... When the money came, nobody wanted to be in the studio writing songs, everybody wanna hang out and fuck bitches... Do the things that they couldn't do when they didn't have money. That kind of killed the business. Cause instead of spending the

money on girls and money, and going all these fly places and dumb shit, you're supposed to reinvest the money in the studio, hire some musicians, play some music... shit I was asking for, they weren't ready. It was a bunch of young cats just happy to be there. And then I started learning, and I started understanding more because I kept going to the label. And the more I went to the label, the more I learned... I learned about publishing, I ended up getting the publishing deal from RuffNation, from RuffNation for $50,000.00. I was making beats, every beat I made I got $5,000.00 for it... I was never one of the struggling Outsidaz. Cause the room was incredible. You knew we would have a hit record before the night was over, because there were so many good emcees. But we never discouraged anyone. If you wanted to try, you tried. If you didn't make it, you just didn't, but we allowed you to try. Know what I mean?

raw *poetic*
+ P FRITZ

TUV: I'd like to start with some history. I'm not sure, specifically in your case Patrick [P-Fritz], how long you were apart of this story, but if you have things to add here, by all means – jump in. I've been a fan of the art here since the Panacea days, but certainly knew of Raw Poetic as an individual and have been an avid follower since Redefinition Records was really becoming solidified. I think the first record I bought from you was that *Kilowatt V1.5* with the 7". I remember I bought it because of Damu the Fudgemunk, but it's the release that made me really pause to think about the art of Raw Poetic. But that was Redefinition Records. And since then, Redefinition has really become one of my most heralded labels. Easily among the most consistent of the last 10-15 years. But before Redefinition, you guys were rocking with a label - that I'm really not too familiar with - and that's Neosonic Productions. Can you fill me in on the story of Neosonic Productions?

Raw Poetic: So yeah, **Neosonic Productions** was **K-Murdock's** production company. He was the producer for **Panacea**. That's just what he called his production company. As we were travelling in and out of labels, he would just drop that name for his production company but it was all of us.

The funny thing is, is it's been us since the beginning. A lot of people don't know **P-Fritz** very well but P-Fritz has been with me for like 25 years now. On the Panacea records? He's on there. On the guitar parts you hear on the Panacea records? That's P-Fritz. That's been my guy from day one. Even before that, we called it **RPM**. We were all just in college, that's where we met. That's kind of the link all the way through.

TUV: That RPM – that's the Restoring Poetry in Music?

Raw Poetic: Yep.

TUV: Oh wow, so both of you were in that. Can you tell the story of how RPM began?

Raw Poetic: Yeah. So, it was my cousin and I, we started a band with some friends; **Drew**, **Aaron** and we had a guy **TJ** on guitars. TJ left one summer and our friend Aaron said, "I know this guy named P-Fritz. I think you're going to like him on the guitar." And he shows up with his guitar… and I had no idea what to expect but I heard him play and I knew at that moment. I said to myself, "I'm going to be playing with this guy for a long time."

P-Fritz: [Laughs]

Raw Poetic: I will say this, every group that I've been in, from Restoring Poetry in Music, to Panacea, to working with **Earl [Damu the Fudgemunk]**, if I'm playing, P-Fritz is with me. That's just how I go about my musical journey. He's my brother in music. So…

P-Fritz: Yeah, when I was in college, I studied music and for me, I started out playing in small group jazz combos. I ended up playing with the guys that Jason was playing with and we were in each other's orbit but we had never met each other but we all knew the same guys. When that summer came, I just graduated college, I didn't have any gigs and I had just moved to the DC Area. It was like, "hey, do you wanna play in a hip-hop band?" Like, "yeah, let's do it." I feel like that kind of thing, in one way or the other, has influenced the sound. It's not like the mix of jazz and hip-hop was anything that we created or is brand new to the genre, but that's had an effect on I think everything we do as we go forward. It's not the only influence, by any means, but that kind of jazz mentality in terms of the harmony and performance and improvisation, that's all there. Not really so much on the albums, but it definitely shapes the live show.

TUV: Yeah, you can say that jazz and hip-hop has had a blended history over time, and obviously there's truth to that, but there is something unique about the way that you approach things. Often times jazz elements are used within a hip-hop structure, and this often feels like the other way around. Jazz becomes the emphasis. Perhaps you can talk about something like Guru's *Jazzmataz*, but even then it's not nearly to the same effect.

P-Fritz: I think it's just like a different way in. You raised a good point, and I'm not sure why that is, except for that, and this is just my opinion, but it's not quite as polished. Jazz isn't my first musical language. There's only so much I can do with it, and I'm not a keyboard player. The type of jazz that interested us, I think collectively, I think was stuff that was not always so structured. If there's a type of jazz that leans more in a neo-soul direction, none of us really had those chops, or that experience, or the ability to sing that stuff, and so we just took it in a more of a fusion-ey type direction. Where my history of listening and playing as a rock-guitar player and I have two degrees in classical guitar as well, so that influences things as well, but some of the best rap groups I've ever heard are groups that Jason hipped me too. So when you stir it in that way, I think it kind of comes down to the voice that's unique to us and our little special way.

TUV: Do you guys immediately start then working on *Dream Awake*? [the RPM record.]

Raw Poetic: Yeah, when we met I think we played, what? Two or three gigs that summer? Then we started working on *Dream Awake*.

P-Fritz: Yeah, a few of those tunes were already in rotation. I haven't listened to that album in a long time but I'd say half of those things were things where you and **Marlon** had already done.

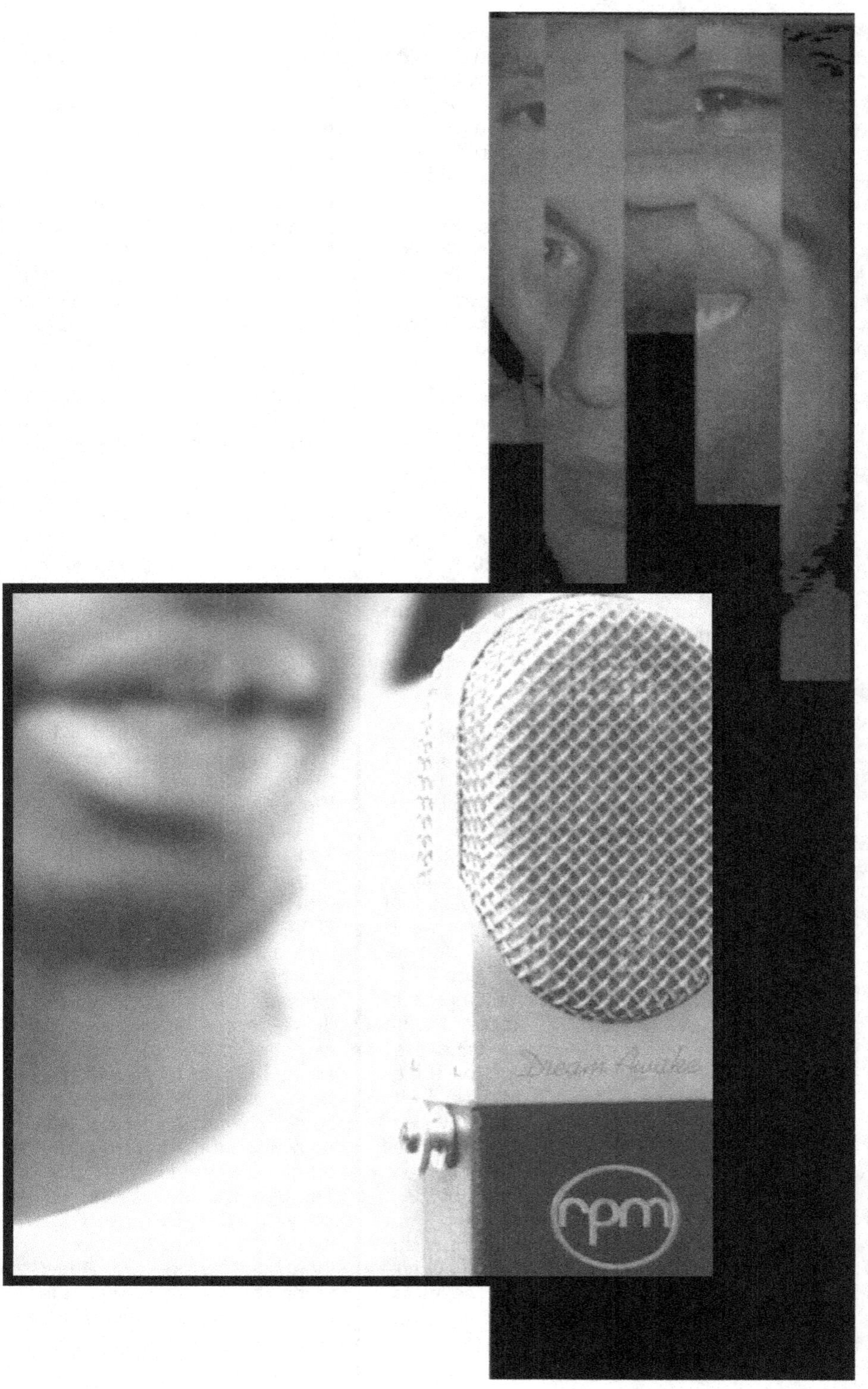
Dream Awake
rpm

Raw Poetic: Yeah, we were already done some of the tunes and were passing them off to the band, then Pat [P-Fritz] came with *Poetry Bum*. Which honestly I feel like was the birth of our sound. I think when we did *Poetry Bum*, I think that's when we saw like, "okay, this is what we need to sound like together." It's when we really started creating. Cause some of the joints that I was doing with me and Marlon were more traditionally hip-hop based. Samples, and you know… Then we would add the band to it to add certain parts. But *Poetry Bum*, I felt like had the full band sound that we were going for.

P-Fritz: Yeah, that was the beginning of discovering our voice as a collaboration.

TUV: I feel like once the Panacea stuff started dropping, the underground started paying attention to what you guys were up too. But for the Dream Awake album, correct me if I'm wrong, it's like 2004-2005, around the early infancy stages of when Panacea dropped. But how did that 'Dream Awake' album do? Did it circulate around the underground scene? Did it do well for you guys?

Raw Poetic: Umm, *Dream Awake* was more… I think locally we were doing alright? But then Panacea was… Well, I write a lot. And I think all my friends know that. I write a whole lot. So we weren't ready to do another album because we were still doing shows for *Dream Awake*, and Marlon had left the group and K-Murdock had joined Poetry in Music at that point. And he had beats of his own and wanted to do a little side project. So Panacea came about by just being a side project. It just so happened that it got picked up by a label in California. **Glow-in-the-Dark Records** with **Jaysonic** and all those guys. So once they picked it up, it was just bigger. Just on a bigger scale.

P-Fritz: Yeah, for a while it was blended because the tunes that **Kyle** and Jason were writing together, we would play some of them in the band, and the beauty of trying stuff out in the band is you get to play it in front of audiences and see what works and what doesn't work. So for a while, you couldn't really discern a difference. The composers were differ-

ent but the group that played them on the record were the same group of people.

TUV: You had mentioned Earl's name earlier. When did Damu the Fudgemunk join this picture?

Raw Poetic: It was all around the same time. Damu showed up at an RPM practice way back. He was only 17 when he showed up. He showed up and he started talking to us about all these records, and we're just like, "who's this guy who knows all these records?" And next thing you know, sometimes he would fill in on drums if we couldn't find a drummer. Sometimes he would be on the turntables with us at the shows. Our group has always been good with people just kind of walking in and out. We had our core members but he was always just part of the family. And then once things started to evolve, people started going separate ways, that's when Damu and I went and did the *Kilowatt* project. He called me up one day, was like, "can you do a couple of verses for some songs I got?" I was like, "sure, of course." That's just how we do. And that's how it transitioned into what Damu did over the next decade.

TUV: Can you talk about that transition to Redefinition Records? I've always just thought of it as Damu's baby, but I imagine there's more to that.

Yeah, it was more of Damu's thing. Damu and a guy that he works with over there. I got more involved in **Redefinition** around 2011-2012 I think. Once the last Panacea record had came out, my grandmother had passed at that time, and then my aunt had passed. It was just about two years where I didn't record anything. I had just kind of stopped recording. I had to do some soul searching with those two things happening. It was **J Nota** from Redef that had played me some songs, cause we had recorded the Kilowatt's stuff a couple years earlier and then he came to me to ask if they could release it. Through that process, he was like, "I'd like to get you with **K-Def**, can you do a project with K-Def?" so I did the record with K-Def and then I did the one with **Kev Brown**. So I just started doing records with them. Even without Damu. Then Damu and I did a record. I don't know, Redef is a weird period, cause now I

have gaps. Cause even after that, I did those three records and then I didn't record anything. I just stopped recording again. I was going through my own life changes.

Damu just always pops up like a genie. Two years later, he's like, "hey, I got a beat for you. Rap on this beat." Like, "okay…" and next thing you know, I'm diving back into it and Damu and I are on a whole other excursion together. So yeah, Redef I was kind of in and out. When they would call me for a record I would do it. You know?

TUV: Patrick, what's your involvement in these records? So if a record comes out and it says… let's say *Laminated Skies*, *Laminated Skies* comes out and it says Raw Poetic and Damu the Fudgemunk. Materially, what's your involvement in a lot of this stuff?

P-Fritz: So I wasn't involved in any of the Redef stuff at that point. At that point I was just trying to get different parts of my life together. Grad school… I had met my wife at that time doing all that… But with the Laminated stuff, Jason and I weren't playing that much music together for a little while, or really any that I can remember. And then Jason was starting to make these albums and he was like, "hey man, it'd be really cool if you could come over here and play on some of these things." I'd be like, "yeah yeah yeah yeah yeah…" But eventually, I remember the *Laminated* sesh, you

just came over, I brought all my stuff, I set up the microphone and over the course of about three hours I just played over everything that he played for me. Like, "hey, check this out…" I'd just play with it, go with it, and try stuff out. Then I walked away and didn't think about it for… I don't know how long it took that album to come out, maybe another year? And then Damu had got his hands on it and I heard the whole thing in it's entirety and I just remember sitting in my car, coming back from a lunch break and I just sat there in my car and finished the album. I just couldn't believe what I was hearing. Cause the song-writing had improved exponentially, and with the combination with Damu, I just never really heard anything like that. That was continuous from beginning to end. And Jason had taken my guitar parts and chopped them up and used them the way that he wanted too… And left some of them completely alone, and that's when I started to get really interested again and made creative space in my life to continue doing this, cause it's the best. It's so much fun.

TUV: Yeah, that evolution, that sonic progression… You said you never heard anything like that, that continuous motion all the way through the record. I do think there's something that's noticeably different from say the records done with Kev Brown or K-Def – *Concentrated Maneuvers* or the *Cool Convos* record. Going from those records in 2015 ish, down to

Laminated Skies, it feels as though there is a totally different approach to the way that the art is created. Those earlier records are really really dope, and they have everything I look for in a dope rap record, but it feels more like a traditional rap record compared to something like _Laminated Skies_ which feels like this beautiful like aural piece of art... It just feels different. I'm mentioning 'Laminated Skies' a lot, but I think a lot of these more recent records, let it be _Space Beyond the Solar System_, or this new record, I think you've carried a lot from what appeared on _Laminated Skies_, forward into some of these newer sounds. Can you talk about that change of approach? Is there even a change of approach to how you make these?

Raw Poetic: Oh yeah, there's totally a different change in approach. The main thing is, between 2008 and when did _Laminated Skies_ come out? 2022?

TUV: Yeah, last year. It was my favourite record of last year.

Raw Poetic: Yeah, throughout that time I practiced instrumentation. I took lessons on how to play instruments, and I practiced producing. Then Damu would come over and we would trade ideas on production. So, _Laminated Skies_ was essentially all my ideas. I wrote all the music for the stuff, I wrote it and then the funny thing was, I was scared to call Patt for

it. Cause I just didn't think what I was doing was good enough for him. You know? So I kept it for a while and then one night we were talking and he was like, "if you ever need some guitar parts, just call me." And I was like, "Okay, if you can come over for a few hours, I'm just going to play some stuff and you play too it... I'll take care of the rest." And he did it, and when he came over, for me, even before I started really producing it, I was like, "this is the sound that I have been dreaming of since I was a kid... I know this is the sound that I've been dreaming of, I know what this is!"

So now I knew how to produce a bit and once I gave it to Damu, Damu was like, "yeah, this is it man, let me add some flares to it." And he came and he laid drums on it and stuff and helped mix the product. And when I went to put it out, I was still nervous to put it out, I was like, "I don't know how people are going to perceive this record, because it doesn't sound like a typical hip-hop record." And I don't think it is... but that's always what I wanted to do. Was make songs that are not stereotypical. That are different. And hard to explain. Hard to categorize. I don't know, I think we just finally caught it. Since then, we've just been trying to find new ideas and not sampling... If anything, just sample ourselves rather than sampling other people.

P-Fritz: Yeah, I'll add to that from the outside. From watching Jason's progression over the years, from when he started making beats until now, and in order to qualify this, I think a lot of guitar players, who I wouldn't necessarily call 'great musicians,' if that makes sense, so they might be very good at playing the instrument but in terms of the global picture, maybe not so fluent in that language, and I think Jason in the beginning... was the best rapper I know, or ever had the chance to work with, but I wouldn't necessarily say that he was thinking of the music in that huge picture, or necessarily had that vocabulary. And you can hear in some of those earlier albums that you were just mentioning, like he started to sing on the hook, and he started to experiment with some things, and I think at a certain point he turned a corner and it's now like him and I are starting to talk the same language in terms of musicianship. For me, as far as my relationship with Jason, I still go back and listen to the old hip-hop records in terms of bolstering my literacy with that, and that helps me be able to communicate. Now I'm starting to understand the history of his language in that music. So that's my take on how these things are starting to come together. It's like we're speaking more of a common language because our backgrounds are starting to become similar.

What do you think Jay? Is that fair?

Raw Poetic: I think that's totally fair man. I think that's the main thing. I think we're always learning from each other. He does things and sometimes I'm rapping and I can tell his guitar is locks into the record. Hearing him do his style, I try to bring it back to him. It's like a ping-pong of ideas and I think now… like now Pat and I are writing a song together. It's just drawing from it. It's like something we planned 20 years ago and we left alone, and we came back and it was the truth. You know?

That's kind of where we are right now.

TUV: Patrick, are you working on rap records outside of the records with Raw Poetic?

P-Fritz: Nope. Nope. [Laughs] I don't have access to a certain degree. I don't think when people look at me they think hip-hop. When I'm out playing gigs and stuff it's the same thing. I mostly work in jazz now in terms of my performances and gigging and stuff like that. I play mostly jazz. But I also like the relationship I have with Jason because it's not going to be necessarily a rap record. I don't mean that in 'just a rap record,' I mean, we don't go in like, "let's make a hip-hop record." We rather go in like, "let's make some music." And we just see where it goes. It all just melts together. So far we haven't had any plan. The one coming out has more of an 'inside sound,' and the one after that is going to be a little bit more 'outside.' Kind of like how *Laminated Skies* was a little bit more 'outside.' But outside of that? We aren't setting any ideas in motion, just let's see how it goes.

So that was a long-winded answer to your question, but no. I don't really have any ties outside of Jason and Earl.

TUV: Jason, you had said that when you were preparing to release *Laminated Skies,* that you were scared to put it out. You weren't sure if people were going to receive the record well. Now that it's been out for some time, how do you feel the reception's been? I love the record. But it's also a record I don't hear talked about too much. But from your end, especially within your own fan community, how have people taken a liking to *Laminated Skies?*

Raw Poetic: For me it's been great. Of course, I always want more people to listen to it or whatever, and I think when people actually see it live, I think they're going to gravitate towards it even more. I think that's what we really like to do is play live music and bring it to the people. But my fear was more around, I know Damu had some certain core fans, and I didn't necessarily want to alienate his fanbase. Cause I know my sound is just different. Damu has his own sound and I have my own sound.

It's just different. I think to this day, a lot of people think it's produced by Damu. And it was like my production, so I didn't want to mess up what he had going on.

In terms of me? I'm just who I am. Either you dig me or you don't. I was kind of cool with it. I just want people to see it live.

TUV: The live element. I have never had the pleasure to see any of you perform in that setting. When you play this record, do you play it straight through? Front to back?

Raw Poetic: Um, the whole record and some of the new record? And whatever Pat and I get a chance to work on. We have so many songs at this point, we kind of got to pick through them and try to come up with a good show.

TUV: And is there always a full band on stage to play it?

P-Fritz: Yeah, we're at an interesting point and this kind of gets to your question. With the evolution of the live performance, in the old days it was all live instruments then we started working in the samples. It would either be me or somebody else playing the samples live. And with this next iteration, it's gone from the three of us – Damu, Jay and me, and Damu's carrying a lot of the weight in terms of he's running the drum programs and the basslines and the samples, and I'm playing guitar and Jay is doing his thing… the next level that we've been working with and performing with now has been adding a drummer back in. So we're kind of circulating and bringing more musicians back, to bring it back towards more of a live element. I think that was one of our strongest strengths honestly was the live show. We're kind of working our way more toward that. But because of the setup it does kind of determine what kind of material we were able to play. So certain tracks are going to sound better with a live drummer than other tracks. Some tracks just sound more complete to my ear if they were just almost played in a traditional hip-hop way – two turntables and an emcee. So that factored in. Like, "how are you two going to translate?" If we were going to try to play anything off of *Space Beyond the Solar System,* … actually, we do, but it doesn't sound like it does off of the record because there's no way you can do that! That album is a masterpiece of production and it's either, you're going to do it with an orchestra or you just are going to have to leave a lot of those tunes alone. [Laughs]. At least, that's the way I see it now.

TUV: A few years ago there was a record that was put out with Archie Shepp. Jason, you're uncle… Right? For *Ocean Bridges*?

Raw Poetic: Yeah! We were all on that one too.

TUV: That's a pretty combination of characters. How did that happen?

Raw Poetic: Yeah man, I went and saw him at the **Kennedy Center** one day. They were honouring him at the Kennedy Center. And my mom and I went backstage, cause that's my mom's older brother and she was the orchestrator of that… she was like, "ya'll two need to work together. I've been telling Jason to ask you for years…" So, he was like, "yeah, sure!" And when we left, I didn't call him… because… he's **Archie Shepp**! I'm not going to bother him. But then my mother called again, like, "I thought you were going to work together?" and this time he actually made plans to come and so of course, I called the old RPM guys… I called Patt and Aaron and was like, "guys, do you want to play a record with Archie Shepp?" And they were all like, "yeah!" Damu was super down for it. Luke Stewart was into it… So we just got a whole band together and they came, and Patt can respond to that because they actually recorded in the

studio. I recorded all my vocals afterwards… but they came and they played it and I took what they played, chopped up different parts and I started rapping to the parts that they let me play on.

P-Fritz: Yeah, that was… that was incredible. That was a highlight of my musical life for sure. Damu played drums on most of that and between him and **Luke Stewart**, Luke is just a pillar of the music community in D.C., kind of the tip of the sphere of the jazz community, and those two guys just drove the sessions. Like a freight train, and the rest of us just filtered in around and he did his thing. And we did that for about four hours. And Archie taught us one of his tunes which was really cool. That didn't make it on the record in its final form and he had already recorded it anyway. But then Jason came back a couple months later and was like, "here are the tunes…" and it just… in my head, exploded. That was something that I've never heard anything before like that. And the energy… It makes the hairs on the back of my own arms stand up when I hear that stuff. Whether I had anything to do with it or not, it doesn't really matter. I just find it very powerful.

Raw Poetic: I felt like more of a character on that album. It feels like when I would get my guys together and they just play? I feel like that's some of the best stuff that nobody ever hears. I feel like *Ocean Bridges* was that. It was just what I wanted. I just wanted my guys to sit there with my uncle and just play. Don't overthink it. Just do it. And it was those moments that just lose you. When you walk into a session with your favourite jazz players and you don't know what they're going to do, they don't know each other, but they start playing and you feel this thing that feels like unlike anything you've ever felt. I felt like we finally got that on record. Like, "here it is. I got it." And to be able to rap over that? For me was a privilege. I was like, "okay. I can put together the best thing I can possibly do over this stuff." So yeah, that was a really fun experience.

P-Fritz: Yeah! And it's a sign of jazz that I've never heard blended in with hip-hop. I don't listen as wide as a lot of people, but that kind of music that's driven by energy, in that way, I really don't know how to put words to it. But to

OCEAN
BRIDGES
ARCHIE SHEPP
RAW POETIC
DAMU THE FUDGEMUNK
REDEF
CONCEPT
RDF150

hear that mixed with hip-hop, I felt like is something kind of revolutionary to me.

TUV: Yeah, for me, from the outside, I too feel that. I think it was the Archie Shepp record that really shifted that direction into this new leg of the career. I listen to a lot and it really did feel new. It felt special, and these last string of records I think have carried that tradition.

Raw Poetic: Yeah, it kind of goes back home for me. *Ocean Bridges* brings it back home but in a totally futuristic way for us also. Cause I feel like it's what we set out to do with RPM. We started off as a band. I mean, college kids, I was going to GMU, they were at JMU, and we were dabbling around with doing live hip-hop groups, the only ones we knew of at the time were The Roots... But in Virginia, just being from this area, if you play music, for the most part, you're playing in a band... You don't have a lot of assets of people that just have turntables and mics, you know? You have band people. So we were trying to figure that out back then. Looking back to *Ocean Bridges*, fast forward almost twenty years later, and everybody has their own experiences and playing all over the place now. This just kind of came over, like "wow, this is it!" We're finally back on to what we was doing. So even back with the production, now we're producing things the way we want to make now. Besides Damu, I'm not working with too many traditional hip-hop producers now. I'm working just with my core who I've always been with at the end of the day.

P-Fritz: In the early days, we were too hip-hop for rock clubs, and too rock for hip-hop clubs. I remember just kind of lamenting that... When people would come and hear us they would be like, "this is great! I don't know what to even call it!" Like, yeah, it's 'music...' but it could be an issue with us when it came to booking shows. And now, if we flash forward, I think Jason's right, now we're just older... And we're kind of stabilizing our lives. Like, "alright, we're not going to try to be anything for anyone, other than just the best versions of ourselves." That definitely I think turns out the best result.

TUV: You guys are putting out a record in

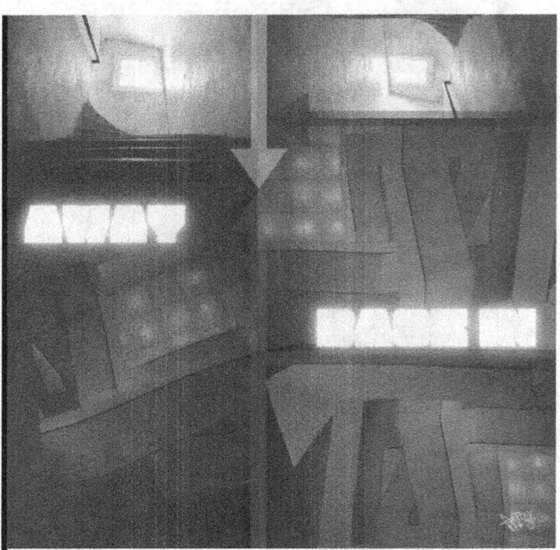

about a month's time called *The Way Back In*. I've had the pleasure of hearing it and it's fantastic. Pat, you described this earlier as an 'inside record,' whereas the next record after this is set to be more of an 'outside record.' Can you elaborate on what makes this an 'inside record?'

P-Fritz: So, I think this one, in my mind anyway, and it's a collaboration so my thinking is only half of this, but we spent a lot of time together last summer talking about these tracks and how to arrange them. So when they were originally written, or the ideas were sparked, I had a couple of Damu's drum beats and just every night I would throw one on and I would play to it until I found something that I liked. And when I got a collection of those, I don't know how many there were, I just sent them all to Jason and he processed them really fast and sent em back. He chose the ones he thought were good. And then we're left with just a whole pile of ideas. The harmony is not super challenging? That's part of what I mean when I say 'inside.' The harmony is just not super challenging to listen to. Trying to think of 'contrast.' And then the structures of the song, I felt personally, allowed them to be structured in more traditional ways. At least some of the singles and stuff. There's like a 'verse-chorus' kind of thing that goes on there. Now, there are some tracks on there that have very non-traditional flows, and when I think of an album like 'Laminated,' I feel like a lot of those songs the traditional song-writing structure just kind of breaks down. But to its own benefit. It gives you that flowing feel. Like you don't know if you're in a verse or a chorus. You're just in part of this vibe…That just continuously stems out. That to me is what I call, and it's not a real precise definition, but that to me is a little more 'outside.' Because the structure isn't in that conventional format. So this *The Way Back In,* I feel might have a wider reach to certain people who maybe aren't always as comfortable with unconventional song structures and harmony and stuff like that. I don't know if that makes much sense, but that's how I think about it.

TUV: Jason, how are you defining this record?

Raw Poetic: Pretty much the same way. I think this record, when we started making this record, I thought, "this is the Pat record." You know?

P-Fritz: [Laughs]

Raw Poetic: It's like, if you look at *Space Beyond the Solar System,* that's the Damu record. *Laminated Skies?* That's the Jason record. This is the Pat record. All the same guys working together, you know what I mean, but this one, like he said, Damu gave the

drum beats, Pat played the guitar and bass on stuff on it, and him and I got together, I wrote the rhymes… and one thing that's so unique with Pat's thinking, and was special to me, I just wrote the songs, and I just free-write, two verses, no hook, a bridge at the end, and he'll take parts and be like, "dude, this should be in the chorus, why don't you use it as the chorus?" So we would try it in the chorus and be like, "oh, that does work in the chorus…" So we were just listening and matching so many ideas, it was such a good record for us to really… like this is the first time that Pat and I were able to sit down just me and him and literally work it out. Like, sometimes… it's never arguing, but sometimes, like "really? That's how you see it?" and we go back and forth, maybe put it alone for a couple of days, and then come back, like "okay, we're back to work, I think we got it."

I looked at this record like, "okay Pat, we got to do this. We're fucking killing this together." So yeah, this was like a record of completion for me. For us, and what we do. Like, now we've come full circle, we're like the two heads of state here and we got the idea to put this together.

TUV: Conceptually, when you go into a

record like this, do you have a concept or a content structure to play with lyrically? When I listen to a joint like this, or really any of the recent output – I don't typically walk away with a core conceptual meaning. I walk away feeling the vibe of the record. The sound, the aesthetic, the imagery, it all becomes the dignifying characteristic of the album. Normally I think that'd be an albums weakness, but here I think that personality is so well dignified it works. But conceptually, how do you go into these?

Raw Poetic: Speaking lyrically for these verses, and even others, I think when I make a record, I'm just in that record. In that bubble. I don't think it's like a concept, I think it's more of a feel. Like, *Laminated*, I don't know, when I think of *Laminated Skies*, I just think of colors. It's vibrant. Soft spoken stuff. This one, I feel like it has a more serious tone. I think there was a lot of things going on when I wrote it. I was a little bit more upset about things, and I was talking about more social issues on this one.

I don't necessarily have a full concept in my head. I don't know, I haven't done a concept record in a long time.

TUV: I have two favourite songs off of this new one. I genuinely love the whole project, but there's a couple stand outs. That's *Sometime After Midnight,* and *Rehab.* Are we able to take a moment to talk about those records individually? We can start with *Sometime After Midnight.* If you have any stories or anything associated with it. But what can you tell me there?

Raw Poetic: Yeah, *Sometime After Midnight*, that one, that Ahmaud Arbery situation happened. I don't know if you know about that situation.

TUV: I do.

Raw Poetic: Yeah, that had happened and for me, being Black in America and being pulled over by a cop, and having guns put up to your head and stuff, seeing that happened with people who weren't even cops, I was just very angry. I just didn't know how else to express myself but through my poetry and rapping

about it. Yeah, you address the situation. Then you go about your day like nothing matters, like it doesn't even phase you. Even though somebody lost their life so senselessly. And we have to pretend like it doesn't even phase us. A lot of people pretend it doesn't happen, or don't believe it happens... So I think that's what I was expressing on *Sometime After Midnight?* Just trying to balance those two parts of your personality. The anger of seeing that happen to your people, and then the anger of having to pretend like it doesn't exist.

P-Fritz: What about *Rehab?*

TUV: Yeah, what about *Rehab?*

Raw Poetic: That one, I believe, is the one where everyone looks at rehab as something for drugs and addiction, and there are so many things that we are addicted to that have nothing to do with drugs. That are not positives in your life. And it was like, "let's try to shift all of that stuff away from us." To try to get back to who you naturally are without it. That's something I struggle with. I see kids struggle with it at a young age. I work in a lower-income community, and a lot of kids, they want the Jordans, and it's all about the flash, and all this kind of stuff... So how do we pull ourselves away from that, and why do we let ourselves get addicted to these materialistic things at such an early age? I wear Jordans all the time. I'm a product of my environment. I wear Jordans because my mom couldn't afford them when I was a kid. And so to this day, I still wear Jordans because now I can afford them myself. You know? So, these things are in my head, like, "okay, how do we strip this off?' So the song is about getting away from that and trying to connect with who you naturally are.

TUV: I can't thank you enough for going through some of these stories are. The new album, again, *The Way Back In*, comes out in about a month's time. August 25th. You were already talking, at least idea wise, about the follow up album, the 'outside' joint. When can we expect that?

P-Fritz: Yeah, we're going to try something out with some tracks on this record. And that's what we're working on when we get off this call, but a big part of our writing style and practicing style and just general style is, there's always a guitar around, is acoustic stuff. So the song Jason referred to earlier, *Poetry Bum* was an acoustic guitar rift and we would just sit down and work it out between the two of us. So these songs from Away Back In are all guitar driven songs, they translate really well to acoustic versions of these songs. In order to shed some light on that process, and that part of our artistic expression, we're going to release a couple of those as acoustic versions. I have no idea how they'll do, or how people will even care about them, I think it's pretty unique to us? I'm sure there's people out there doing it, but again, when you hear it, it has our stamp on it. So that's the next thing. I don't know when that will be, but that's the next thing. Before the next 'outside,' record.

TUV: Amazing. Again, I can't thank you guys enough for going through this with me. I've been such a fan for so long. It's an honour to be able to have this conversation with you guys. Thank you.

P-Fritz: Thank you, man! That means a lot.

Raw Poetic: Yeah, thank you for the interview. We appreciate it.

TUV: Let's start from the beginning. Where exactly are you from? Ohio?

OLO: Yeah, I'm from Akron, Ohio.

TUV: Whereabouts is that compared to say Cincinnati or Columbus?

OLO: Okay, it's about two hours away from Columbus. Probably, depending on the traffic, it's maybe like 45 – maybe an hour away from Cleveland. It all depends.

TUV: How old are you if you don't mind me asking?

OLO: I'm 27.

TUV: 27, Okay. So growing up in that area, were you aware of the local scene that was going on in Columbus? Cats like Blueprint and Illogic? Greenhouse Effect? The Scribble Jam in Cincinnati? Were you aware of the local scene?

OLO: Damn, you're kind of putting me on. I didn't know that. This is just a little bit of info about me, but I wouldn't say that I was sheltered growing up? But I was very to myself, just naturally. On top of the fact that I just followed what was given to me growing up. So I just listened to what my mom's played. I didn't really have sense of what a music scene could have been, or if that was even a fucking thing. Until I moved to Seattle, I never knew of a place having any scene, that was all new to me when I moved out here back in like 2016.

TUV: Did it feel different in Seattle then, compared to where you were at?

OLO: Oh, definitely. It feels different. But when I went back home I realized that there is a scene. And well, to some very very small degree I'm part of it, but I think that was the reason I was never really 'in it' like other people. Just because I didn't know of it. I was just trying to make the music that I like to make, so I never really made music that people around my area kinda made. So I just didn't know how to assimilate myself with those people. So to keep it all the way a hundred, I never really thought of it until I moved to Seattle, and that's only because people from Seattle flew me out here and tried to get me introduced and stuff like that.

TUV: So you end up moving out to Seattle in 2016, at that point are you already making rap music? Is that already part of your life?

OLO: Yeah, I've been rapping ever since I was like 4 or 5. But I used to just do it for myself. And in third grade, my teacher was like, "when ya'll get done with ya'lls work, ya'll can write a poem, draw a picture, write a rap…" She said it just like that, and I think it's because she realized that she was in a class full of black kids and trying to connect with students, but she said it and I remember the feeling. Cause it started like in the middle of my back, and it shot up to my left shoulder, up through my neck and right to my head. When she said that shit, something just snapped in me. I was like, "holy shit, I never thought of it, but you do have to write raps. I guess you would have to write it if you go and make it a song. Cause what I saw on TV was just music videos and I'm like, "these niggas just know lyrics out of nowhere?" Like as a kid, as a young kid, that's how I picked it up.

TUV: [Laughs] Just the flyest mother-fuckas around.

OLO: You know? So yeah. I had always been rapping and when she told me to write in the third grade, that's when I started writing. And I had notebooks on top of fuck-ing notebooks. The story that every rapper gives. I had a whole bunch of notebooks or the shittiest raps, but they meant a lot to me. And by the time I was like, 13? 14? This dude that we just ran-domly met, cause my mom used to sell cheeseburgers [laughs]

and this nigga was buying food from us one time and my mom started talking, just hanging out, and me being the child who was always able to speak with adults, we started having a conversation. And he seen that I had an x-box. And he was like, "what do you want for that X-Box?" I said, "what you got?" and he said, "I got a computer." So he gave me his computer and I don't know what happened one day, I was just thinking to myself, "there's gotta be a way to make music on this thing… there's gotta be." And then I stumbled upon FL Studio and freshman year I started making beats. By sophomore year I started making beats that I was more comfortable with. I just started making music as soon as I got into high school pretty much.

It just continued on from there.

TUV: So what were you listening too at that period of time? You said a lot of your music tastes comes from your mom's, you talk about watching music videos on MTV, but what was your pallet?

OLO: Like around when I started making music on the computer?

TUV: Yeah, 13-14, when you trade the x-box for the computer.

OLO: Okay, every MP3 player had a rule. The absolute rule was these five artists had to be on the MP3 player and whatever was in their discography I had to have. So it was always **Eminem, Kanye West, Lupe Fiasco, Nas** and then it would probably be **Jay-Z**, but not even because I listened to him, but because I thought I had to have him on my shit. I didn't really listen to Jay-Z. Like, the person who made me want to rap, is honestly? **Lil Bow-Wow.** [Laughs] But Eminem was the first person I looked up too. I was just like, "there is no way he puts words together like this." Back then, I never paid attention, and I don't know what's wrong with people these days, but motherfuckers be all sensitive and shit. But the shit that he said back then? If he were to say that shit now he would absolutely be hated. But I thought all of it was funny.

I was like, "he's obviously not really doing it." He'd be in jail… He's obviously not this evil satanic being… He's being hilarious! So to me it was just funny. I don't care what nobody says, if you can make music that's also funny, you're hitting two different senses that people love. Which is the joy of music and laughing? Ah bro. You're doing it! Like you're fucking doing it! So I always thought Eminem was funny. So it was always Eminem, Lupe… Lupe especially. Loved Lupe Fiasco. Kanye kind of…

TUV: In referring to Eminem, I think the humour is what captivated me to the cat as well. And the fact, that by the Eminem Show came out, there was like a real passion to his delivery. It wasn't just humour and punchlines anymore. It felt like he was talking to you. I had never heard hip-hop or music that felt so powerful, so commanding. I was also a kid, but it meant something to me.

OLO: Eminem Show was the one with *Toy Soldiers* on it correct?

TUV: Nah that was *Encore*, the next album. Eminem Show had like *Square Dance, Sing for the Moment, Hailies Song*, etc. The main single was *Without Me,* it had like *My Dad's Gone Crazy*, all that stuff.

OLO: *Cleaning Out My Closet…*

TUV: Exactly.

OLO: As a kid, to me, I've always been fascinated by words. That's how I started 90% of most of my projects. They start from a word. And it took me until I was an adult to realize that. And I think I had a problem admitting that because I thought it was stupid. But the older I get, especially with the way that I believe, as of now, I realize how powerful it is that every idea that I've ever tried to bring to life, or have brought to life, it all started with a word. Being the fascination of the word, the way it sounded, what it meant, where the word came from, the etymology of it, all of that. Those were things that people like Eminem or Lupe, especially those two, they would always get me with just the words… Sometimes I'd hear certain words and that would spark ideas for me

to write my own raps. So those were definitely people that I always looked up to a lot.

Then of course **Snoop Dogg**, and I feel like Snoop Dogg had the one cheat code that a lot of people don't got. Like where singers have beautiful voices, he has the greatest speaking voice of all time. So his rapping voice is just phenomenal. Don't get me wrong, he can spit too, but Snoop Dogg's power was that he felt like he could literally talk his way into selling you the clothes you're wearing. Just from speaking. He don't even need to lie… He can just be like, "you need that shirt nephew…" and you're like, "you're right… How much?", "twenty." That's why I always loved Snoop Dogg. Cause the way you say something to people, your voice… **Pop Smoke** had that same effect. Your voice matters. I always admired that. So yeah, Snoop, Lupe, Eminem, Kanye West, and Nas…

And the reason I actually listened to Kanye West before I even liked his music, is that I just considered him one of the "Black artists." Like you know, one of those people that are 'for black people.' Nas and Kanye were people I made sure I listened too cause I felt like I needed to ingest it. Once I found out that Kanye was the one producing a lot of his own shit, that made me fall in love with Kanye West. That one fact changed everything. That was pretty much my list.

And then when **Tyler the Creator** came out, all of that shit changed. Tyler, **Earl**, freshman year, I think 3-4 months into freshman year, Tyler and them dropped… but yeah, that was what I listened to around that time.

TUV: So how do you go from that pallet and those influences on the stuff you're making now? The earliest material that I heard from you, I think it was 2017, with *Super Pisces Robot Kingdom*, and you can definitely see growth from that album to the new one that you just put out, but even then, it doesn't sound anything like the cats that you're talking about here. It doesn't even sound like Odd Future.

OLO: I appreciate that, that's a good thing.

TUV: 100% a good thing.

OLO: The way I look at music, for instance, I always go through certain phases where I'm making rules on how I listen to music. How I ingest it. What I want to listen too, and things of that nature. I don't listen to music to copy. I don't listen to music for motivation. For instance, the song that **Drake** had with Jay-Z, *Light Up*, right? Literally my favourite **Drake** song of all time. As far as I'm **concerned**, Drake has never made a song to match it. The cadence of it, the beat, the flow, the everything… every time I hear that beat drop, right before the beat drops, when that chorus comes in? I get chills. Every single time. Me talking about it right now, I'm low-key getting goosebumps. That song? Is something that inspires me to make something that can do that to someone else. I get inspired. I don't believe in motivation; I believe in inspiration. Right? Inspiration is when something happens to you that makes you want to do some thing. As where motivating you, you're letting someone make you feel so bad that you get up and do what they're telling you to do, or you follow someone else's advice because you seen it work for them. Inspiration is supposed to drive you to do something. It can be similar, it can be adjacent, it can be extremely different, but it's because I get inspired by the people I listen too… I'm not really a 'fan,' I'm not a 'fan' of people, as much as the music inspires me. I'm not a good fan, I'm not a

good 'fan boy,' I don't do stuff like buy merch, I don't represent other people's ideas, I can't let you into my world, but I can tell you with a straight face and with respect and love that you're the reason that I added my art to my world. You're the reason that I paint my world this color. That's why I think my music sounds the way it does.

TUV: **There's a word for that physical response, that physical reaction when you listen to music. When it transports you**

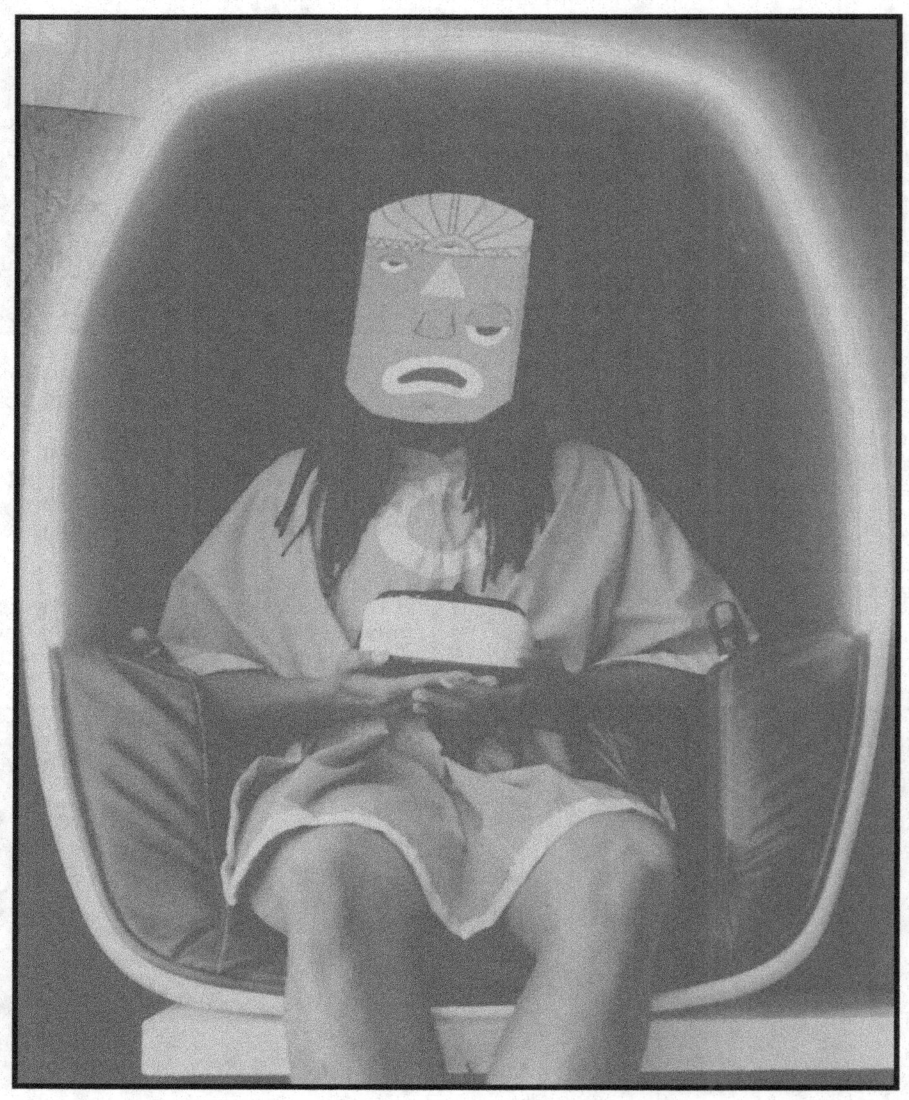

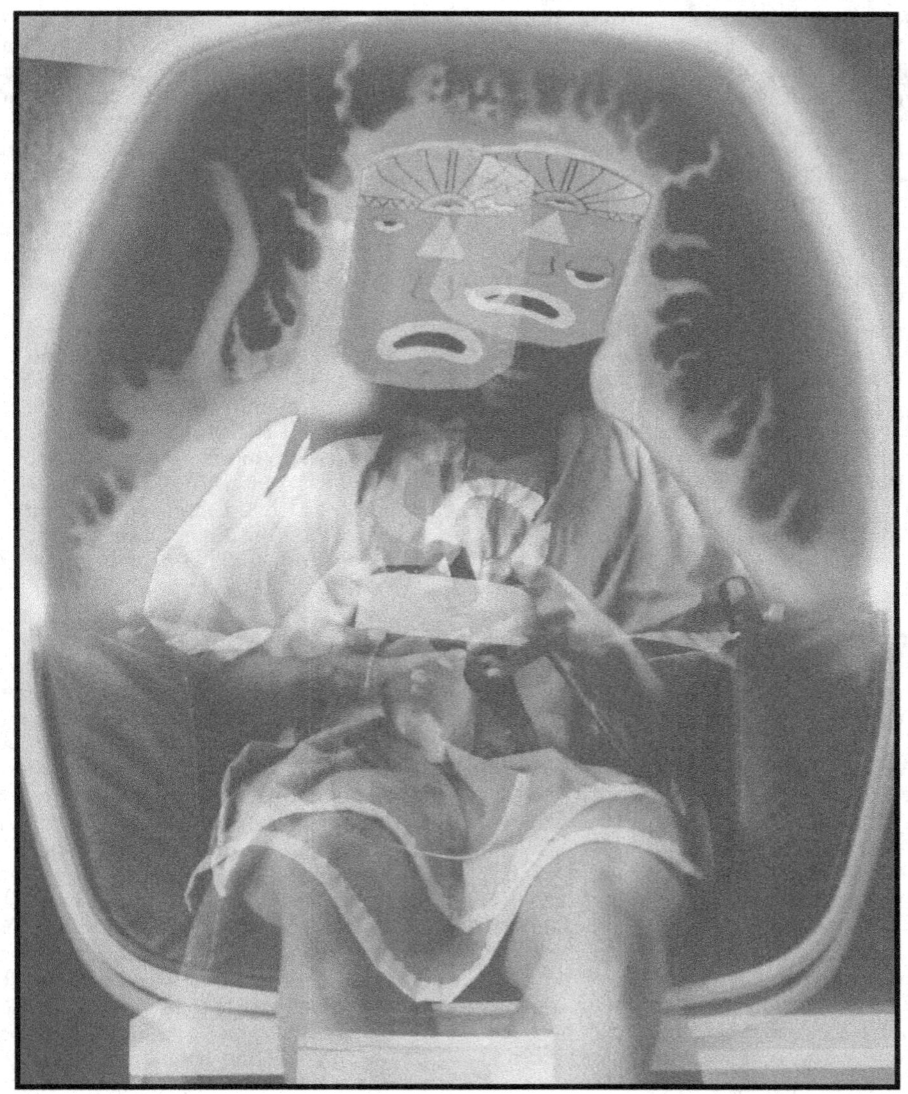

into that moment. When it leaves you with that sense of awe. The word is 'frisson.' If you look up the term 'frisson,' it'll say, "also known as aesthetic chills." There's something so powerful there. I think you're right. I think that's why I seek out art and music personally. It's to capture that feeling of frisson. I'm a fan of artists, but I'm not a fan boy. I don't obsess over the creator, but I admire the feeling that the art gives me. That frisson is what I'm chasing.

OLO: I think I have seen that word. The reason that I choose inspiration over motivation or even imitation, is because when you're inspired from somebody, that's when you're truly able to innovate. My big thing is, even though people tell me not to focus on it, I love to do things... not differently? But in a way that people know for a fact that 'I' did it.

TUV: The other album that I heard, so I heard *Super Pisces Robot Kingdom,* I heard the new project *AI Chimera*, the other album that I heard though is *Light ! Ray ! Beam!...*

OLO: That's my baby.

TUV: I'm not sure if it's the origin of it, but at the very least the front cover shows you spotting that mask. Are you able to talk about the mask at all?

OLO: Yeah.

TUV: Who made it, the origin of it, what it means to you?

OLO: Well, as I'm looking at it right now, the mask is one of about thirty different iterations of what it could have been. The reason I chose this one is because in the art of it itself, it just represented a lot more. With the eyes being placed where they are, from the pyramid in the middle kind of giving them a sense of... not necessarily direction, but perspective? Right? The entire character of Lordra is he's like an omni-kinetic hyper beam. He exists in ways that people can't even fathom. The mask is pretty much what fuels him all together. It started out as just an emblem. At first, he was just an emblem and then he grew as I grew. As I grow, he grows. The mask... We all want to do things the flashy way. And at

one point, I will, and I don't know how to transfer the energy from that mask to the next one, but at one time I will be getting a new mask, a new iteration over time. But I wanted to just put the costume into reality, or it wouldn't be real. I would just be every other person making music. I wouldn't be an actual artist living their art. How when you see people who would rather starve and paint all day, and then they finally make their magnum opus or whatever, like you're living to create your art... That's what matters. All the other shit to me is extra. So, one day I was just like, "I'mma do it myself." I grabbed a piece of cardboard from an Amazon box, I cut it out, I drew on it, I painted it, and I was like, "huh, this works." It was just a logo before, so I was like, "you know what? We're doing this."

My sister crafted, I guess you'd call it either a poncho or a gown, or whatever you want to call it, she's the one who made it for me. I designed it, she made it. I chose colors that I don't typically like at the time. Green is never a color I cared about. Pink is also a color that I didn't necessarily like. And I didn't like those colors until I used them on the outfit. And I chose colors that I didn't like so that I had to embrace something that wasn't me. Cause that's when you get to see how truly powerful you are.

In the sense of being Lordra, I'm always in an outfit. I would never never ever choose. But I make it look good and I do my fucking thing in it. You can't tell the difference. Lordra is all about power. It's not about controlling people, but it's about power. Not power over others, but power at all. You know? That's what the mask represents, just power. Where power comes from... you have to grow your power. You have to realize your power. And you have to radiate your power. Meaning you have to be able to release it. Not necessarily let go of it, but how to emanate. How to exercise it. How to show your power. So that's what the mask is. I finally put it together and we did a photo shoot, I had the homie Passive Lens, that's his name on IG **[@thepassivelens]**, he came over from Kentucky to do a photo shoot with me and we were just in the woods. I just felt everything was looking so natural, the costume alone made it look like I was in a foreign place. I either wasn't on Earth, or a place that at least wasn't in America. I realized

how good it came to life, and I just let him live. So that's what birthed the dawning of the costume and the mask and everything else.

TUV: When you make the art. Do you make it under the guise of playing a character? Or is directly from yourself? There has to be something of yourself regardless, but is there a thought or intentionality of a character?

OLO: It depends. I'll say this, if I'm in costume, I don't know how to say it in any other way, other than when I'm dressed up, I am Lordra. When I am not, I'm who I was born as. Who I've grown to be. So, when I'm in costume I'm definitely in character. There are times where I try to put myself in the mind space of Lordra, and that just isn't something I can do all the time. Cause when I'm in that space, that's what I consider to be my highest creative space. It's when I'm able to freestyle the best. It's when I'm about to flow the best. It's when I'm able to emanate all of the art that I want, the way that I want. It's when I can take something that I just wrote last night, perfect breathing, all of that... When I can finally execute an idea for the upcoming comic. And I can get the idea in a perfect line and be able to write it down. When I can look at it and say "that was perfect." That's when I'm in the mind of Lordra. So, I don't try to do it, but certain art for certain things require as-

sistance. It's similar to when you go hunting. You don't necessarily think the same way that you would when you're at work, because you're in a different environment, doing different things, and you expect to see a different outcome. So yeah, sometimes I am 'not me' when I'm doing art, most of the time... A healthy amount of the time.

TUV: That's a really beautiful sentiment. This idea that the costume is your environment. If you want to change your environment, you can change your get-up. You can change the way you present yourself. And that in tune acts the same way as changing your environment. The costume is your environment that you're occupying.

OLO: Have you ever heard of a game called **Cardfight!! Vanguard?**

TUV: No, not at all.

OLO: It's just funny because they have this new mechanic where you 'overdress' your character. Basically, lay another card that's probably stronger over the character. Basically, giving it the ability to power up on the field. I just feel like it's interesting the way that you described that back to me. Cause it's kind of like that. Your universe is inside of you. You have trillions of microbes living inside of you and they depend on you to be a healthy universe for them. The only way that I can imagine having a universe to change, is to change its motion, its direction, and its intent. And sometimes the best way to do that is to change the way that you look. So that the way that people look at you, changes the way that they react to you. It changes the way people respond to you. It changes the way people treat you. That in term will change the way you move.

TUV: When did you start rocking the mask? Was it the *Light!Ray!Beam!* album?

OLO: Yes, it was for the *Light!Ray!Beam!* album.

TUV: If we jump forward to talk about the new album, *Al Chimera*, it's produced by Khrist Koopa. Can you talk about how the two of you met?

OLO: Yeah, so the homie **Kohl Wright**, shout out **LONER**, the clothing brand in Seattle. I was at his house one day. We were just chilling, talking, cause me and Kohl really link on a mental level. That's my boy. Like we know how to have an actual conversation. So we're at the house just chilling and I think he said something like his friend is coming over, or whatever, just one of his homies… and it ends up being Koop. And me and Koop get to talking and one thing leads to another and he finds out that I made some music, he liked what he was hearing, and then me and him had a conversation and again, he liked what he was hearing. He's a very spiritual person. Spiritual people are very far and few between. Genuine spiritual people. So when you do find someone that you can actually have that convo with at any moment, and actually retain that information and be able to engage in that conversation on a real level? You link. So that's how we started kicking it with each other.

He found out that I knew this rapper named **NoEmotion [NoEmotion Goldmask]** Shout out to my brother NoEmotion, that's my uncle, out in Florida… He found out that I had a song with him and we just started linking once we found out that we had similar interests and shit like that. Over time, just here and there, seeing each other out at different shows and shit, we usually work with the same artists…

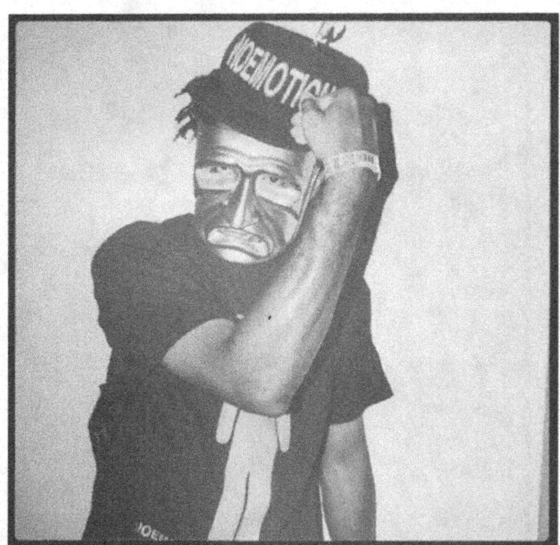

and this one day right before I ended up leaving Seattle in 2018, the last person that I ended up hanging with was actually Koop. I was at his house and we were in there making music. Again, we were just talking and having a real ass conversation. So we just became friends.

Then we had a conversation while I was out in Ohio about us working and me being apart of **UDF [Unity Diversity Freedom]** and all this other stuff and it just slowly became what it is now. When I came back in November of last year, I just got right too it. Cause that's what I was supposed to be doing, I was supposed to be out here working.

TUV: I love it. It's not very often you run into cats who know who NoEmotion Goldmask is. You run with some cool ass people man. Speaking of NoEmotion, but he's another one that does the sort of anonymous mask-wearing persona.

OLO: Yeah man, NoEmotion was the first person I ever bought music from. Like real talk, we were broke growing up. So every Eminem and Snoop Dogg CD I had was a burnt CD. Even when I got them for my birthday. It meant the world to me, I just wanted to hear em, but when I had some money, and it was money I got from donating blood when I was 18-19, I bought this project and it was called the *NoEmotion Gold EP*. It was this flash drive that came with like five albums. The posters, stickers, cards, all this other shit. And I used to just show it to all my friends and we'd sit there and laugh at all of it. Cause it was so fucking funny. Like, dude this guy is fucking dope. And then he'd be really saying real ass shit! We'd just be sitting there, like, "did you hear this?" So I had everybody listening to NoEmotion for a little minute because he was just that guy.

So yeah, I found out about him, and I was just like, "that's my dude. I fucks with him."

TUV: Returning to the Al Chimera project – when do you begin to work on that? And it's credited to just yourself, as a Lord Olo solo project, but what was Khrist Koopa's involvement here?

OLO: He was the producer and executive producer. If I'm being 100% honest, we were supposed to just do a project together. But then I was just like, "let's just make it like a UDF thing, whatever happens happens… If this is involved with UDF, let's just rock it. Let's make the album dope. Let's make it a UDF project to throw that shit back out and get this bitch spinning again." He ended up producing most of the tracks. He was intending to produce all of them but low-key, and he'll probably tell you this too, I'm admittedly, I wouldn't say 'difficult' to work with, but I'm picky, I don't like rapping to the same vibe of music track after track after track after track. It pisses me off and I feel like I'm listening to one long ass song that never has a fucking orgasm at any point. So I was just like, "I need to co-produce some shit, I need to hear some shit." So I started throwing some beats in

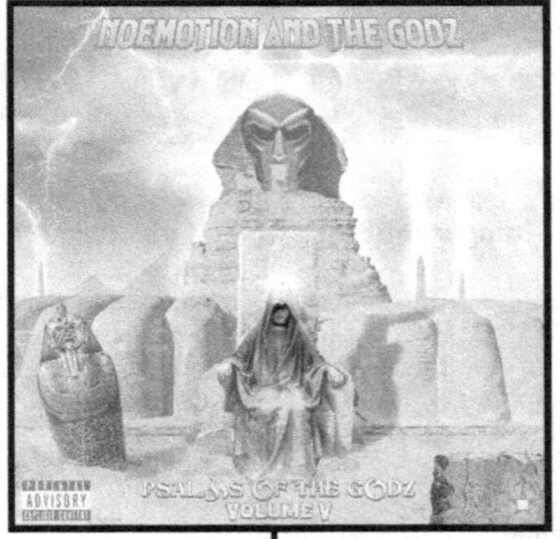

there… Then the homie **Televangel** reached out. He reached out to Koop and he sent me some beats. I was like, "are you fucking serious? DOPE!" So then I was like, "alright, put him on the project." Then there was also a song from **AJ Suede** which I recorded to… He gave it to me back when we had this whole debacle with a venue back in 2020 or something, I can't quite remember. But he had given us some beats after we had recorded the album *Metal Detector Music*. And I recorded to them as soon as I got home like 4-5 days later. So like 5 days after I made the songs or whatever but I didn't release it. I just saved it, and as we were making this project, I was just like, "this may fit." We didn't even know what to call it at the beginning, I just knew what I wanted it to be. How I wanted it to explain itself musically. So Koopa was the executive producer. He set the tracklist, he was pretty much the one plugging me with everything that was going on. I literally, for the first time ever, just got to be the artist. I only had to rap. That never happens. I usually have to take care of everything that I'm doing. Hell, I would call him the director. He was all of that.

TUV: I have a few favourites from your catalogue that I've heard that I'd love to dive deeper into.

OLO: Let's go.

TUV: The first one I believe was my introduction to you as an artist, as it was the single – but that's *Charisma*. What can you divulge there?

OLO: Me, Khrist and Wish Baby was at Koopa's house and Koop was playing me beats. We were all just jamming out, finding shit, right? And he plays this beat and at the time, me and Wish was talking about maybe doing a project together, right? And I told Wish when I heard that beat for *Charisma*, "I want this beat, but I'm only rapping to it if I can rap to it by myself. I don't want to share it. If you want it enough to where you want me to share it, I'll just let you have it. But if I'm rapping to it, I need to rap to it myself." And he was like, "okay cool." And bam. That's pretty much *Charisma*. When I started hearing all those little keys in it, I was like, "I need that." That was really the vibe I was looking for. The over-active but extremely rhythmic drums... Just popping off every-where? Like, "yeah, I'll set this off." And yeah, Koop found a really cool place for us to shoot the video. Like, "this works!"

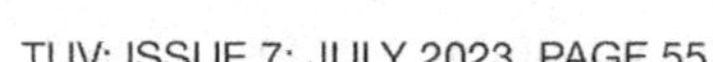

TUV: I wasn't sure which other one to choose here from the 'Al Chimera' joint, but it was either between Eyes Up or 'War', but let's go with 'Eyes Up'. Do you remember anything about that song?

OLO: Yeah, that's the one that AJ Suede pro-duced. That song was part of another project that I actually made and disbanded. So a lot of the songs from that project will be in other projects. But the project was basically about my experience coming back to Seattle. And just how much it had changed from when I left. So I made this whole album basically expressing that, like seven songs. And two songs that AJ Suede produced for me, *Eyes Up* was one of them. It was just kind of part of that... but that song was just me talking about personal shit. I just wanted to think... It was like a deep breathe for me. That song.

TUV: Maybe in a similar vein here, but I think my favourite song I've heard from you so far is from *Light!Ray!Beam!* and it's *Be Someone*. The second song. Can you talk about?

OLO: That's a fucking fire ass song.

TUV: It's so good. Sooo good.

OLO: That's one of my favourite songs. I wanted it to sound like a song I would have woke up and heard in the year 2001. I sam-pled the song *Swallow from* Bush.

TUV: That was my sister's favourite band growing up! She was a huge fan of Bush, Silverchair... that kind of scene. I heard that shit so many times growing up as a kid.

OLO: I love that song. Every time I would hear it though, I would hear *Swallow*, and I would get these clash feelings because I was having a nostalgic feeling from how it sounded. It sounded just like the 2000s. But the image that would pop in my head was all the people I met and knew in Seattle. Al-ways just self-victimizing and self-diagnosing themselves, doing all kinds of drugs, shit like that. It just made me think, I don't know if these people are weird, or are in trouble, or whatever, but just the ecosystem... that's just how it was. Or at least that's just the imagery that I got from it. So yeah, as I was making that *Light!Ray!Beam!*, the record was kind of inspired by my mom. My mom used to always tell me that I had a light in me. It was a light that other people wanted. So I have to be careful of who I chose to be around. Who I chose to interact with. If you actually listen to the album, there's parts where you'll hear my mom talking... She's basically continuing a 20 year old conversation that we've been having.

But yeah, *Be Someone* is just one of those songs where if you hear it, you gotta relate to it. Cause it's gotta be true… If it's not true for you, I don't think you're human. I was just being as open as I can possibly be. Giving everything I want from this experience we call life.

TUV: Love it. Like I said, it's my favourite song I've heard from you so far. Let's talk about the future. Are there any projects that you currently have on the go, that you're currently working on, that you are at least able to discuss?

OLO: I think everything's on the table. Televangel already mentioned in an interview that he did that he was working with me. So I guess since he mentioned it, it's fair to mention. But I immediately started working with Televangel as soon as I submitted the album to release. The minute we submitted it, I started working on the songs and beats that he sent me. So that's a project that I'm expecting to happen this year. Given all things go as I'm expecting them too. That's definitely going to happen.

There's a deluxe version of the *Al Chimera* coming out. I'm not sure if I'm going to settle on either two extra songs or six, I don't want to do anything in between, either or. Either two or six extra songs. But yeah, that's like my immediate next that I'm working on.

And then my biggest project, my baby, this is probably the one thing that I want people to care more about over anything… My Kickstarter for my comic book! For people who want to know what it is to experience Lord Olo and his mightiest! The comic book is something I'm working on. My illustrator that I linked up with, he's from South Africa, shout out to him. He's always done great work for me. Me and him linked up a long time ago, we established a great relationship online. And just so he's properly compensated, all the money goes straight to him for illustrations. It doesn't go to me at all. Anything extra is only going to go to the production itself.

If we raise more than the goal, which is 7,000… that'll be great, but 7,000 is the goal that I'm aiming for. And that's the biggest thing that I'll be doing.

GOOD
ACID
jackson

Ill2lectual: I guess a little history on the group. We originally started back in 09'. We did a couple of compilation features with some people around the area, like the long beach area of Cali. And we put together this cassette way back in? I think it came out in 2010? Something like that. Then life happens. So we kind of took a hiatus from things. Our project in particular is kind of like an art project for both of us. So there's no real time frame for anything, there's no real like, "we're expected to crank out this much material day to day, when we get together we crank out what we crank out - but this EP, this was kind of the first time we got to stockpiling stuff and putting it out. So this is the lead in to a full length that's coming out later this year.

We got some things in the works with another follow up already for that one as well. So things are kind of cranking out for this side of things. That's awesome that you heard *Something in the Water*. I sometimes forget about that EP. Did you hear the other one? *A Man Who Thinks With His Own Mind?*

TUV: I don't think so?

Ill2lectual: That's another **Illogic** album. I did that one as well.

TUV: I probably did then, I'm a big fan of Illogic. I've spoken to him…, Blueprint…, love that Greenhouse Effect material. But I don't recall the name.

Ill2lectual: Word.

TUV: So that first Acid Jackson project - were you two going by Acid Jackson back then, 2010?

Ill2lectual: Yeah.

TUV: What was the name of that joint?

Illistic: *High Bias Dynamics*.

TUV: Are we able to take a bit of a step back to talk about your own roots, individually into the culture? Illistic, if we start with you - how did you get into this?

Illistic: I was born in LA. There was always music around in the family. When I was about 5 or 6, my pre-hip-hop was like **Bobby Brown** and **Michael Jackson**. In the early 90s. My sister used to always play like **LL Cool J** and some other acts. That's when I got into like **Dr. Dre** and **Snoop**. That was when my childhood kind of starts, when gangsta rap comes in the late 80s, early 90s. I just kind of always loved the words of it. I've been writing short stories as long as I can remember. I just loved the art form of it.

TUV: Were you immersing yourself in the LA underground rap scene come the mid to late 90s? Even the early 2000s? Cats like Project Blowed, LA Symphony, were you at all hanging around those crowds?

Illistic: When I got into like high school, one of my closest friends he started putting me on. Cause I was really into the mainstream, I didn't know the underground existed. Probably around 97-98, I got into like **Planet Asia** and **Hieroglyphics**. Early like **Eminem**, pre-**Aftermath**… I don't think I listened to **Project Blowed** until I got a little older.

TUV: I want to ask the same question here for Ill2lectual. Where's your roots in this?

Ill2lectual: Oh wow, so I'm an old man… Honestly, **The Beastie Boys** kind of kicked it off for me. Once that hit though… There was little tapes like **Spice-1,** some **Eazy** [E] cassettes that you would hear from people, but when Beastie Boys kind of blew up, it was like, oh, it's a little different having that 'wow' 'booming' 808s hit ya. You know? From there, it was just trying to get your hands on as much as I could. I was a kid, you used to collect cassingles back in the day and put them in my shoe boxes. Look at them like baseball cards as a kid. As things floated around, from the mid 90s and what not, there was a lot of back shit out there that was still kind of cool - your **Kid n Play's**, your **Fresh Prince** and stuff like that, but what really kind of got me going big was in like 92 ish in the area, the mobile DJ became a real thing. In the area that I grew up, I was really fortunate to see people like **Beat Junkies** do their thing. They were floating around the area going from house party to house party. It was kind of like that movie *House Party*, where you'd have that ride filled up with records and turntables and you're going to somebody's house when your parents are gone and you're doing it up. So it was kind of neat seeing cats like that come up. And then flyer parties started getting real big. So you had groups like **Cypress Hill** and **House of Pain** and **Doobiest [Funkdoobiest]** doing their thing and getting really big. At the same time, you had a lot of small underground cats doing just as big but in a more localized level. You know?

TUV: **Do you guys ever remember going to the Elements hip-hop night in LA in the mid to late 90s? I spoke to DJ Bonds and Breeze a couple years who ran the night together - and it would have been around that same time.**

Ill2lectual: Nah, I didn't go to stuff like that, I was more of a little loner, skater, graffiti kid. So when people was doing stuff like that, I was the dude out and about kind of spraying. [Laughs]

TUV: **Fair enough! What about yourself Illistic?**

Illistic: Umm, no. I was kind of an introvert too. It's kind of funny because we both are. But I was more into collecting what I could find.

TUV: **Ill2lectual, you talk about graffiti and spray paint. Did you have a graft crew at this time as well?**

Ill2lectual: [Laughs] yeah… but I'd prefer not to… [laughs]

TUV: **That's fair!**

Ill2lectual: I was real heavy around the freeways. On like the 901 / 605 area. Stuff like that.

TUV: What region of LA are we talking about in terms of you guys growing up?

Ill2lectual: So we're at completely different areas. I'm over in like Long Beach area, and he's Palm Dale. Hell, it should only be like an hour away but it takes like two and a half, three hours…

TUV: So how did you guys link up with all these Ohio cats? The Blueprints, the Illogics, etc?

Ill2lectual: Umm, well, I'm friends with **Kristoff Krane**. I did a couple of remixes on Kris's, I think they were called *Mixxy's* or something like that? He had these… man, he had a collection of them! I think he did like eight or nine all together… Something like that. Anyhow, I met Kris, geez… A while ago. Man, I met him a long time ago. They were touring, I forget which tour I initially met him on, but we hit it

off. He was just around, geez, I think every time he came to Cali for a minute. He'd stay at the house… and from there, working on these remixes for him and then, you know, we've done a couple of things ourselves. He put out that *Fanfaronade* project, and I remixed a **Buck 65** track originally that I think a friend of Kris' was a big fan of his… So he ended up doing the remix for the release and then my first choice was Illogic but somehow it was like, "oh, that's taken…" So I got a Buck 65 track, and then it turned out *that* was taken! So I got my wish! And came onto the Illogic track. So I did a flip of that and that was kind of my initial step into meeting Illogic and chatting with him. I think I started sending him beats. It was going to be like, "hey, let's do a single." But we ended up putting out that *Something in the Water* EP instead. A few years later we did another full length. So Kristoff Krane essentially is what helped make that leap in there. He introduced me to **Jordan Miche** and we did a little project called

Floating Feathers, back in the day. And from there, just other people staying on tour and swinging by, staying at the house and what not… you just meet these people. You hit it off with them you know? Like-minded people. Dope shit like dope shit.

TUV: Gotcha, and Blueprint would have came through Illogic and that whole scene?

Ill2lectual: Correct. Yeah.

TUV: Are we able to pivot and talk about this EP? You guys take a long break, and you talked about that hiatus early on, but what was the impetus to re-combine energies and put out this project?

Illistic: Like he said earlier, we had a lot of life things going on. At a certain point both of our fathers passed away at the same time. We had kids, not close together but we had grown up a little bit. Coming back together happened when I moved out to Las Vegas from California. I took my first real break in actually recording there. Right before Ill2 had moved, I got with him and we just kind of started talking from there. The chemistry never really died out.

TUV: Now, Illistic, I'm not too familiar with your back catalogue. Were you actively recording during this interim period? Do you have solo records out?

Illistic: I've only released one. It's an album called In Search of… Right after that I got with Ill2lectual. I knew people in the LA scene, would do performances, things like that. But when I got with Ill2, it was kind of like… I call it a boot camp. Cause I wanted to elevate to another level as far as my recording, my writing and my skills. So we kind of really really took a break from whatever we had going on and really just focused on him. So when we did our stuff in 2009. After that I went to school to be an engineer and got my business degree and things like that. So I wasn't releasing material until I got my affairs together.

TUV: So when it comes to this EP here, and well, you're calling it an EP, but this is a meaty-EP… Right? It's not like a 3-4 track thing. 12 tracks. A couple interludes

Kristoff Krane
fanfaronade
Produced by Jaq

thrown in there. But you said that this is gearing up to something later, and that you're doing a series of these things. Are you able to talk about the plan for the future?

Ill2lectual: So we essentially, we're sitting on... two other full length albums already in the pocket. It's just a matter of how we want to dress them up and arrange them. How it's going to be presented... The EPs, essentially the EPs are going to be EP - full length - EP - full length - EP - full length. The EPs are all going to be a little bit interconnected in a way, just by way of each EP is going to make up a part of one single phrase. I always thought it was dope when I was a kid when I had my cassettes set up on the side if they all made up a phrase or a wording of some sort... Sometimes I would try to see if I could plug them together that way. But anyhow, over time - once all the EPs are out, you'll have them all stacked together and it will say that entire phrase. It's kind of a nod to my boy... I used to do audio for **Strictly Cassettes**. My boy Mark brought in this artist, **Koreatown Oddi-**

ty, he does a lot of work with them still, real sick artist... but anyway, K-Town was doing this beat tape to every year in the Chinese calendar. So essentially, it would be like a ten or twelve year project that's going to roll around in that calendar. So he has a beat tape for each one. So each beat tape is connected by way of that calendar. So I thought that was always tight. So it's kind of a nod to the Strictly Cassette crew and what not.

TUV: What's your vision for Acid Jackson as a group? What do you guys want for this thing? Or is it just making art and seeing where it goes?

Ill2lectual: We're making art and seeing where it goes. This is essentially for us. Music has changed over the years. For me, there's a lot of wack stuff out there. Not that my shit is anything great, I'm sure a lot of people think my shit's wack but... when you're able to make your own, it's dope. So we've kind of made this for us. Now it's like, let's get it out there and see what happens. We don't have any real... We're not trying to blow up. Matter of fact, I kind of didn't want to put anything out. Illogic helped kind of push that over the cliff a little bit with support of people like him, I guess it's like, "shit, I guess I gotta put this shit out, let it shine a little bit." I keep a pretty low profile.

TUV: You guys picked 'Sit Alone' as the first single. Can you talk about that decision?

Ill2lectual: I thought it highlighted his lyrics pretty well as an re-introduction. Like, "we're back, we're here…" We kind of feel like we're in our own lane. Meaning, I don't think we sound like a lot of other groups that are out there. So I feel like that was a nice little nod to introduce him to everyone.

Illicit: That song has a lot of meaning to it as far as that particular record. I won't go into super specifics, but that record in particular was kind of like a jumping the hurdles kind of moment for us as a group, so it has a special meaning behind all the layers of the lyrics.

TUV: The name of the EP is *Good Grief.* You said that the titles are interconnected in some way, do you have the titles already mapped out?

Ill2lectual: Yeah, I got the names already for the EP - that's part of that phrase. It's not like it's anything crazy dope ridiculous. It's not like it's a phrase where people are going to be like… "oh my god…!" It's nothing like that, it was just something I was like, "yeah! That's dope!" So it's being done that way. But the full length? That's going to be called *Own Your Own Shadow.*

TUV: Are you able to talk about that full length at all? I've listened to the EP, is this going to be an extension of that sound?

Ill2lectual: You want to say anything on it Ill?

Illicit: I mean, you're going to be getting more. For us, it's about the quality of the record. So anything that we put together as far as sound and direction as far as us? It's not going to ever get to you guys without me or him being dead-set on these. I might hear something, he might hear something…

Ill2lectual: As far as the sound, yeah. You can definitely expect dusty spacey sounds. There's a couple tracks on the EP which are like three-part songs in a way, they change up… So there's more of that going on in the full length. I'd say it's sculpted better. It's a lot more sharper; the full length.

TUV: Beyond the Acid Jackson stuff, as musicians, I imagine you're working on your own endeavours as well. Can we talk about some of the solo work that's on the go? Maybe we can start with you Ill2lectual?

Ill2lectual: Yeah, yeah. I got a new album that's going to be like the first of like four. A collection of beat tapes that I'm going to be putting out on cassette. The first one should be this winter.

TUV: Do you have a name for that yet?

Ill2lectual: Not really, but the theme of it is going to be seasons, so I believe their just going to be, like *'Spring,' 'Winter,' 'Fall,'* depending on how I want to attack it.

TUV: And what about yourself Illicit?

Illicit: Yeah, my plans as far as releasing projects is once this EP and LP drops, I'll be releasing an EP in the Spring of 2024 and it will be called 'Effect.' I'm trying to take the same approach as we're doing with the Acid Jackson, EP-LP, and just try to scatter them around. I'm not trying to pollute what we're doing with Acid Jackson.

TUV: Aww man, I'm really excited for these feature joints. As I said before we began, I came into Ill2lectual through the work with Illogic and I'm a huge fan of this sound. I'm excited for anything you have on the go.

AJCKS
Acid Jackson
GOOD
GRIEF

An e-mail conversation with Danny Veekens.
Founder of Rucksack Records.

TUV: Let's begin here, do you consider Rucksack a label? Or more so a 'vinyl distributor'?

DV: I definitely see **Rucksack Records** as a label. Vinyl is our preferred format of choice, for sure. But there's much more to that than just releasing music on wax. Curation plays an important role in that. Our tagline is "Records by mavericks who make heads nod and jaws drop." That's what kinda holds everything together. The productions always need to make people's head nod—hip-hop is always at the heart of what we do. Particularly (but not limited to) beats. But at the same time, we're looking for that impressive and special something-something that also makes your jaw drop—whether that's the beat wizardry of **Spectacular Diagnostics**, the more psych-y productions by **The Expert**, **LTF's** take on Soviet Funk, or **Thijsenterprise's** jazz grooves, among others... If a new release pushes me down a rabbit hole of (new) records or stories to explore, that usually means it's the right fit! I hope the same goes for listeners; that they discover something new each time.

Besides that, I also strive for the right press and promo runs for each release, and to properly tell the story of each release. I usually joke that that's what happens when a music journalist starts a label—that's what I do as a freelancer. On a more idealistic level, I want to support (independent) artists to the fullest. With the right promotion and distribution, not owning any of their rights, fair payouts, and to help them get further.

So yeah, to get back to your question: Rucksack Records is definitely a record label to me. At the same time, to put it more simply: "we just release dope records." [Laughs] I guess that's the higher goal: that's what I want people to think when they see our logo or spot our name. That they're in for a ride and that it's going to be a good record to check out.

TUV: I'd love to dive into the curation process a little deeper, but if we start with a bit of a step back - what do you personally look for in art? You talk about that 'special something' - are you able to unpack that, and try to articulate what that is?

DV: It's indeed quite hard to put into words. But let's give it a go: it's mostly—and that's why I use the word 'Mavericks' in the label description—about artists (mainly producers) who dare to try

new things and/or who push their own art forward. I mean, take The Expert, for example. I'm sure he could've successfully made two or three more laid-back instrumental albums in the vein of 2019's Excursions. But instead, he went for a psychedelic hip-hop record together with emcee **Jermiside**. "Marvin Gaye's 'What's Going On' meets **Edan's 'Beauty And The Beat.'** That was the original pitch for 'The Overview Effect.' Usually, such an overly ambitious pitch makes me raise my eyebrows; I'm sure I even did that in this case before listening. [Laughs] But they surely delivered one hell of an album that fully lived up to those words! Dutch producer **Jelee** is another example: after a couple of sample-heavy beat releases, his debut album **Soil** features all-original compositions, with the music and album sequencing deeply inspired by video game world-building.

That's part of the "special something" I'm always looking for. So with that approach, there's a certain narrative to each release. Stories as a result of producers who push themselves into new realms. It's like you said when we first got talking: an "adventure in sounds." That's what I want to offer a platform and home for with Rucksack Records.

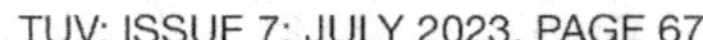

TUV: I feel as though a lot of the music that we're discussing - there's a sense of maturity imbued into it. Even the instrumental cuts somehow seem tethered to an older crowd. When did you start to realize that this is the sound that most resonates with you?

DV: That's interesting. I never intended to tether to an older crowd specifically. But I guess you're right.

For me personally, I used to run a magazine and website called **The Find Magazine** from 2008 till 2021. That's always been focused on a melting pot of hip-hop, jazz, and beats. So a love for that sound was always there. Even years prior to that. But if I have to pinpoint a moment when (in hindsight) a sound for the label started to take shape, it is when I put together the 'Jazzvolution Chapter Two' compilation back in 2019. That's also when the idea of starting a record label clicked for me. In terms of sound/direction, things started to come together. The B-side was intended to be a more jazz-influenced, free-form approach to beatmaking, with more live instrumentation and compositional elements. Especially a track like LTF's **"Kalypso"** was an 'a-ha moment' for me. With that said, LTF also ended up releasing records on the label!

TUV: Let's talk about the label directly. You've talked about the sound and the direction you wanted to take - but what's the origin story? When did you get this thing off the ground and where did you set up shop?

DV: The idea had been brewing in my head for years. Partly after releasing several vinyl records, cassette tapes, and digital releases with The Find Magazine.

The first one was back in early 2012: a 7" by **Mr. J Medeiros** produced by **Stro Elliot**, with a **20syl** remix on the B-side featuring **Shad**. That was huge for me, as I was a big fan of all of their music.

But truthfully, back then I still had no clue what I was doing in terms of manufacturing, mastering, pressing, or distribution. I learned a lot as I went along.

THE FIND
REWIND

Actually, the very first release was a cassette-only compilation called The Find Rewind in 2010. The title was obviously inspired by the movie Be Kind Rewind with **Jack Black & Mos Def**. The tape featured previously unreleased material by the likes of **Suff Daddy**, **Kev Brown**, **Daru Jones**, **Free The Robots**, **Factor**, **Dela**, and **Kero One**, among others. Quite a crazy line-up, now that I'm thinking about it!

The idea to start a label was also fueled by people who kept telling me I should start one, as I was essentially already supporting independent artists via The Find Magazine anyway.

Plus, on a more bitter note, hearing bad "industry rule #4080" stories about labels time after time again from artists also motivated me to start a label to offer the right support and efforts.

Fast-forward to January 31st, 2020: that's when I officially started Rucksack Records. With an EP by London-based producer **Bobby Obsy** (who also happened to have designed our first logo) to first dip our toes in the water. Our first vinyl release was also being manufactured at that time: the **James Crown** 45 by **Kid Sundance**, released in collaboration with **Dutch Gems**. But guess what? By the time that was released, the world went into a global pandemic and full-on lockdown mode...

For the label, I guess that was kind of a blessing in disguise. I ended up having much more time on my hands to build out the label. In hindsight, that also shows in the label's output: nine releases in that first year alone! So to answer your question about where I set up shop: it was basically my living room with me, myself, and I. And my girlfriend. And my cats. Those times in lockdown were weird of course. But it was somewhat of a special time for the label, because so much happened in that first year. The first vinyl releases, first radio plays, press support - seeing all of that come together. But needless to say, it was a weird and difficult time as well. I clearly remember an email from someone in Italy, who reached out to say he was feeling super down and completely isolated during lockdown, but that receiving the record made his day, so he could enjoy new music again. The power of music...

TUV: I love that history. I'm a big fan of a lot of the artists you mentioned, but it's ultra cool to see that the first joint was with Mr. J Medeiros and Shad. I first heard Mr. J Medeiros through the track, 'Pale Blue Dot' probably around then, (2012) and it became a huge favourite. When it got the 45 treatment, I simply had to get it. As for Shad, that's the Canadian homie! I'm so happy to see his success with the Netflix series.

I'm going to have to go back and do my homework on that Find Rewind comp. [Edit, I was just looking it up, and it was the Pale Blue Dot Remix that Find Mag put out! How incredibly coincidental. I fucking love that record. I made a few videos about that shit on YouTube back in the day!]

Can we talk about Find Magazine at all? How intwined are the magazine and the label for you? Do you consider them an extension of the other? I've spent most of my life dreaming of starting a label and starting a magazine - and although I've only pulled the trigger (so far) on the magazine front, in my head, they share the same purpose: to engage in the artist community, help give voice to art I enjoy and to hopefully put others on.

DV: Oh, man, 100%! If I had all the time,

money, and manpower in the world, I would definitely run a magazine-slash-record label hybrid of sorts. You just hit the nail on the head: I also feel like a magazine and record label can share the same purpose. Or at least beautifully strengthen each other. For example, I'm a huge fan of **Grand Royal**, the former label and magazine by the **Beastie Boys**. I also have an **Archie Shepp** record here, with a magazine-styled insert unfolding as part of the gatefold sleeve. Or think of how **Ego Trip's** editorial team put together **The Big Playback** on **Rawkus**. Or the **Test Press Club** series by **Worldwide FM**, which came with pocket-size magazines about the artist and the music. I love such ideas and formats. I'd love to bring something like that into fruition. One day...

TUV: Is The Find Magazine birthed under the same pretences as Rucksack?

DV: Back in 2007, I started The Find Magazine with more or less the same goal to sup-

port and cover (independent) producers and emcees.

More from an editorial perspective, though. As I was studying journalism at that time. But the record label element slowly creeped in by also releasing compilations, cassettes tapes, and that 7" I mentioned.

I started Rucksack Records in early 2020 and The Find Magazine ceased to exist in late 2021. So it's definitely an extension. I simply couldn't do both, also combined with my freelance work. And I have to admit that after running The Find for thirteen-plus years, I kind of lost passion and interest to keep it going. It was time to move on. In hindsight, starting a new label was a sign of that.

So I definitely see Rucksack Records as somewhat of a continuation of The Find Magazine, albeit in a slightly different (perhaps more matured, like you pointed out?) direction.

TUV: Any story on the Pale Blue Dot single? That is still blowing my mind.

DV: First and foremost, shout-out to Mr. J Medeiros for the trust! We featured Mr. J Medeiros on the cover of one of the first issues of The Find Magazine.

Back then, pre-social media, that was still a 'PDF magazine,' free to download via Rapidshare or Mediafire. The good ol' days. [Laughs] It took a few more years before doing a couple of print editions.

I stayed in touch with Mr. J since. I can't recall exactly how the idea of doing the Pale Blue Dot 7" single and promotion together came about. But I do remember that I fell in love with the song instantly.

Mr. J pulled some strings on his end to get French producer 20syl—who he's now closely collaborating with as **AlltA**—on board to do the B-side remix. He then invited Shad to hop on the remix.

To be honest, I'm surprised this isn't a highly sought-after 7" these days. It's such a crazy collaboration. Maybe there should be a remastered reissue one day.

TUV: More people should definitely be aware of that era of Mr. J. Medeiros's

career. A reissue is definitely due! Thanks again for the detail here! Always fun to read.

Let's transition to talk about some of the more recent material Rucksack has put out. So far this year there have been 3 releases - in the case of both Spectacular Diagnostics and Stik Figa / The Expert, I follow those careers already - but the other - Jelee - was completely new to me upon discovering the label. Since that was the first release, can we spend a little time to profile Jelee?

I know the name came up in a previous answer, but I'd love to learn more about who this cat is, and how Soil entered your hands.

DV: Sure thing. Jelee (pronounced as "jelly") is an Amsterdam-based producer. I first got introduced to his music by finding a copy of his self-released debut 7" Yesterday's Art / Paraluna in 2019 at record store Black Gold. Shout-out to store owner **Siebrand** for always supporting local artists and labels, by the way! That 7" really blew me away. I loved how the release showed he had vision—especially for a debut from a fairly young artist—, from the art direction to the productions. Back then, his music was very sample-centered. Clearly inspired by the LA beat scene (and beyond). No surprise that he ended up doing a beat set at a **J Dilla** tribute event as the support act for **Samiyam**. Later, he also supported **Brainfeeder's Salami Rose Joe Louis**... After releasing a series of singles and EPs, the album **Soil** Rucksack Records released earlier this year in collaboration with Amsterdam-based label **Wicked Wax** was his official full-length debut. Fully self-composed this time (with several homegrown collaborations), which was a departure from his sample-heavy sound. The arc of the album unfolds like an adventure video game —besides beats, video games are another huge passion of

his. The cover art of Soil, beautifully hand-painted by Amsterdam's **Charayda Andeloe**, also reflects that concept. The music brings together elements of hip-hop, jazz, electronica, house, video game soundtracks, and more. I really appreciate how he clearly knows what he wants—and doesn't want—with his art. Also for this release. From the music to the cover art idea to the back sleeve's pixel art to the photography for the insert; he had it all in his head. **Lucas** [of Wicked Wax] and I just had to sit back, nod our heads, say "okay," and let him do his thing. Jelee also runs his own record label, by the way. It's called Heliopolis Recordings. That's really worth checking out, very original and conceptual releases.

TUV: I love the sounds of the new Jelee record. As I stated, he was a new artist to my own vocabulary, but certainly owes a deep dive. The other two big releases from this year come from Stik Figa / The Expert as well as Spectacular Diagnostics. You've worked with The Expert in the past - but can we talk about these albums? I'm interested in both the narrative (how they came across your plate) but also, what about these joints made them the right fit for Rucksack?

DV: With both **The Expert** (Dublin, Ireland) and **Spectacular Diagnostics** (Chicago, IL), I can blindly trust that they come up with something crazy and great...

Ritual by **Stik Figa** & The Expert is somewhat of a continuation of The Expert's psychedelic influence on The Overview Effect with emcee **Jermiside**. As mentioned earlier, that album was inspired by **Marvin Gaye's** narrative on What's Going On, mixed with tripped-out beats reminiscent of Edan's Beauty & The Beat. There are a lot of twists and turns in The Expert's beats for Ritual as well. Really lively psychedelic productions.

I've been a fan of Stik Figa since his **Mello Music Group** days and collabs with the likes of **L'Orange** and **Oddisee**. So this was an awesome pairing for me following Stik Figa's appearance on "Black Tears" (one of the main singles of The Overview Effect). With crazy guest features on Ritual including **Blu**, **Solemn Brigham**, and **Defcee** as the cherries on top!

While working on Ritual, Stik Figa actually told The Expert that this was going to be his very last album, which had an impact on the writing and production process. There's an interesting interview with **The Rap Music Plug Podcast** for more on that. Take closing track "The Forgotten," for example, which sounds like a swan song; Stik Figa's last hurrah. That track still gives me goosebumps every single time...

When it comes to Spectacular Diagnostics, there's real detailed world-building on **Raw Lessons.** From the art direction and designs (all-him! The cover art was later brought to life by **Quelle Chris** for the animated video of "Political Monsters," by the way) to the samples to the guest features. There's so much detail and subtle references to discover in his productions. It's insane. Also, I feel like calling

him a "producer" doesn't do him justice. He's more like a producer-slash-designer-slash-A&R. The way he keeps his ear to the (under)ground, shows in the selection of emcees he works with since 2017's **The Spec Tape**. On Raw Lessons, that includes both US emcees **(Fatboi Sharif, NAHreally, Curly Castro, Bruiser Wolf, Illogic...)** and UK emcees **(King Kashmere, SonnyJim, Lee Scott & Bisk, Remi Rough, Juice Aleem**...). Also, wait till you hear his next album…

TUV: What can we expect from Rucksack going forward? What's the vision for the label?

DV: We currently have four records lined up till Summer 2024, which is going to be quite a diverse ride. First up is a double LP by Dutch producer and multi-instrumentalist Thysenterprise, which is very much grounded in jazz. Still with a clear hip-hop production ethos, though. Then there's a 45 record by Russian producer LTF which is drenched in Soviet Funk. And then there are two other albums I can't say much about yet. But I guess I spilled the beans on one of them in my previous answer…

Spectacular Diagnostics
RAW LESSONS
RAW
LESSONS

In the long run, the vision is to keep exploring new directions and fringes. Always with a deep and clear love for hip-hop. But the end game is that the catalog becomes much more kaleidoscopic with hip-hop at its core. Chicago-based record label International Anthem is a huge inspiration to me: they're essentially a jazz label, but they're blurring those lines—you can't really call them a "jazz label." That's how I envision Rucksack Records in the future, yet from the perspective of hip-hop. I have no idea where that's going to take us exactly. That's what makes it all the more exciting.

DISCOVERIES

OBSCURITIES

GEMS

DJ RISKY BIZ - THE SHADIEST [1998]

Stumbled across this while reading old news bulletins on **RebirthMag.com** from back in 2001. **DJ Risky Bizness** had just (as of January 29th) re-released his 'famed' Eminem mixtape from 1998 on CD for the first time. The tape was called *The Shadiest*, and was stated to have 'blew **Eminem** fans out of the water.' I was skeptical I was going to find anything online, but in 2014 - Risky Biz uploaded the joint to Mixcloud and provided a much needed explanation. For whatever reason, the Mixcloud link won't work on my end - but it's since been re-posted to YouTube. So you can hear it.

The story told here is dope. Apparently, Risky Biz from Chicago, was making regular trips down to Detroit to meet up with **DJ Head** - who happened to be Eminem's DJ during the **Lyricist Loung**e / Unsigned Hype era. He is also credited on half of the cuts on the *Slim Shady EP* (either production or drum programming) and had put out an

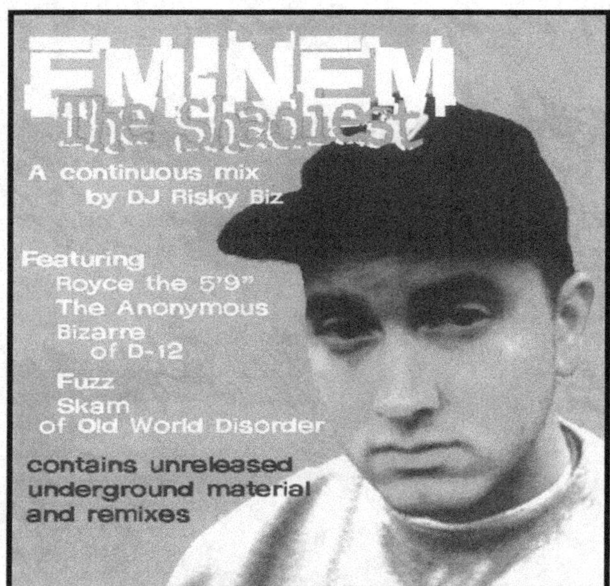

ultra-ill mix with **Proof** back in 96' called *W.E.G.O.* (also available on YouTube.) This was back when Proof was apart of the **5-Elementz** crew. Needless to say, Head had the gems. During these trips, they would exchange cassette tapes and demos - rare MI rap for rare Chicago rap. When word was out that Em was about to sign to **Dre**, DJ Risky Bizness and **DJ Mike Cue** got to crafting the the mix we have in front of us. *The Shadiest.*

This shit is super ill. It's 98' Em. It's all the shit you've heard from the *Slim Shady EP* era. Rapping at the Outhouse with **Bizarre** kind of era. Radio freestyles at **Sway and King Tech** era... What a blast from the past. I remember downloading most of these cuts from Limewire and Kazaa back in the day - and although I would return to the cuts later in life - it's great to have these all collected. Furthermore, the remixes are dope as hell. I actually dig the beat on *As the World Turns* used here over what made it on the *Slim Shady LP*... One of my favourite Em cuts, *I'm Shady* is also I would argue... improved? I love this mix - and to be fair, I may go back to this one more now than the OG.

A lot of people would argue that this was Eminem in his prime. And a listen to this mix is certainly evidence for the argument. I personally will still take the 2002-2004 more impassioned Em - but this punchline version of Em's catalog is where I originally fell in love. The Shadiest mix captures the essence of Em at his rawest.

Plus - there's new ish! Well, new to me. The mix promises some unreleased material and rare demo cuts - and as a long time Em fan, there were rhymes that I simply don't remember hearing anywhere else. I loved this thing and as a long time Em fan (specifically this era), I never knew that this existed. Ya'll should peep this.

"So recently i have had some people ask me about the Eminem Mixtape The Shadiest that i released back on 98 with help from my buddy DJ Cue..i haven't listened to this in a looooong time..lol so i decided to dig it up and put it up here on sound cloud . So here is the story.. back in 98. i was going to Detroit to meet up with Dj Head..trading to get dope Local MI Stuff and i would bring him Local Chi artist. Now head was Eminem's Dj and had produced most of the Slim Shady EP.. Em had already made his buzz in the underground (Battles,Lyricist Lounge,Unsigned Hype) and was recording a new album. When i got to detroit my and Head in his basement talking bout Em's Buzz and what was going down and he said em was bout to be signed i was like word, i was like cool i was like i just got this new gear and wanted to do a mix of some of the underground em stuff.So i drove home with a bunch of demos and figured i would thow them together in a mix tape release and give it out to my homies. i never imagined Eminem or the mix would get big lol. So anyway here it is The Shadiest a collection of rare Eminem Demo's and other stuff you may or may not have heard. Originally released on cassette only (99) , this was mixed together from a combination of Cassette's , Vinyl , Cd's on a Roland VS880 Workstation (Who Remembers those) over two nights with my Homie Dj Mike Cue assisting me and Jeff Fernandez whipping up the artwork back in the day...listing to it now i cringe and laugh a little... because some of the things we did on there i can't believe we did lol,but we were just figuring thing out (apparently i felt a bit from a old SNL record fit the mix lol)- hope you enjoy some of this old stuff." - DJ Risky Bizness 2014

THE LAST EMPEROR - THE INTERSCOPE ALBUM [1998]

About a year ago (June, 2022) - a user by the name of **GoodWilHustlin** uploaded to YouTube the track *Victory* from **Last Emperor**'s shelved-debut album that he recorded with **Interscope** after being signed to **Dr. Dre.** Along with the upload, he posted the photos below which gave us the first look at the track list at Last Emp's never before heard album. Previous to this, the only track I had been aware of from this era was *Airwave Terrorists* (produced by Dre) which featured **Hittman**, and was thought to be a leftover from *The Chronic 2001* (not on Last Emp's solo).

Animalistics was the joint that got Last Emp some credibility around the Lyricist Lounge scene in the mid to late 90s. *Secret Wars'* was also a famed track, with the sequel *Secret Wars Pt. II* being most likely the first track people hear when they're put onto Last Emperor. For *Secret Wars*, Emp pits his favourite emcees against his favourite comic book heroes. Demonstrating all out lyrical warfare on both fronts. Additionally, *Remember* we can imagine is *Do You Remember* - an incredibly potent and heartfelt ballad which stands as a personal favourite amongst the Last Emp discography. In fact, many of these songs were released previously over the years; from b-sides, vaulted-compilations, etc. Hell, *Clear Day* even made it onto *Palace of the Pretender,* with both **Masta Ace** and Trugoy on the cut as guest features. Only two songs on the tracklist are nowhere to be found. *Disappearing Acts* as well as the now-uploaded *Victory* thanks to our friend GoodWillHustlin.

Now, we can imagine, or at least I'd hope, that many of the tracks on the Interscope album would have differing instrumental selections than the surfaced tracks. Although this may not be the case, Interscope did own the rights to the original tracks, and would likely have refused to allow a cut like *Clear Day* to appear on 'Palace and the Pretender' three years after dropping the artist without at least some changes. I wonder if Masta Ace and **Trugoy** were on the original even (they aren't listed on the tracklist. I've dreamt about this hidden album for years. Last Emperor is an all time top 10 emcee for me and this hidden gem has been at the absolute top of my "albums I wish I could hear" pile since day one. I hope the whole Advance becomes listenable at some point. But for now, enjoy *Victory* - shit's beautiful.

... CONTINUED: WORDS FROM Q

How did we get signed to Dr. Dre? That 'how' question, is a process question. And it involves other people. The story essentially goes, Last Emperor and I, Jamal Gray and I, we met at Link University in Pensylvania. We graduated in 1995. During that time, we're recording and we're doing shows. One of the shows or open mics that we did that was popular at the time was the Lyricist Lounge. The songs that the Last Emperor was writing were like no other. Some of the most popular songs were 'Monumental,' 'Meditations,' 'Animalistics,' and 'Secret Wars.' 'Animalistics' is what Dr. Dre signed him for. And 'Animalistics' is also what garnered Jamal - The Last Emperor - a quotable in The Source Magazine. Which was something that was very big. Most lyricists, that was a coveted thing… to actually get a quotable in The Source. So we got that, and Dame said, "Ayo Q, let me get a demo from Jamal and I'll get it to Dre." I didn't think anything of it. Dame had went to school with us, his name is Dame Johnson, we called him Dame Dollas. So Dame gets our demo and gives it to Dre. It's interesting, Dame's brother is Philip Atwell and Philip Atwell was doing videos for Dre at the time. Of course, we didn't know that, but that's how our music got to Dre. So we got signed by Dre.

What happened was, we go out to LA and Dre is sitting at the boards at Larabee Studios. So Jamal and I are at the back and 'Animalistics' is playing, and Dre is reciting the music… We're just looking at first, like, "yo! this is straight-up Dre! I can't believe it." Now mind you, right before we get out to LA, Tupac was murdered and then Biggie was murdered. We got signed in 97', in April. So here are two east coast cats coming over to the west coast. So we didn't know what was going to happen. We just knew that we were on some social conscious music. So we were just going out there to do what we do. So that's how we got to the attention of Dr. Dre. That's the how.

Why did we leave Dre? The 'why' question - and that's something that you'll all have to ask yourself at some point in your life - what is your why? Why did we leave Dre? We wanted to put out music. And Dre was taking relatively long. And whatever his process was, or however he viewed putting out music, it didn't fit our 'why.' We wanted to put music out. We thought that we had material that if he just stamped his name on it and came out with the singles, that he was obligated to give us, then we would be fine. But as history has shown, he takes time putting out his music. And unfortunately time waits for no one.

So I wrote a 3 page letter to Jimmy Iovine, explaining why we wanted off of Aftermath Entertainment, and it was no disrespect to Dre, it was just he was taking far too long to put out music. And at the time, we signed before Eminem, Eve was on the label as well. She opted to get out of Aftermath and go to Ruff Rydaz. And we were still on Aftermath. And we opted to go to the parent company - Interscope. The interesting thing is, Interscope wasn't the type of label that was putting out, I guess what you'd consider it at that time, 'urban music.' So you'd put out your music on these 'boutique' type labels, that's what they were calling them. So you had Ruff Rydaz, you had Rico Wade, I

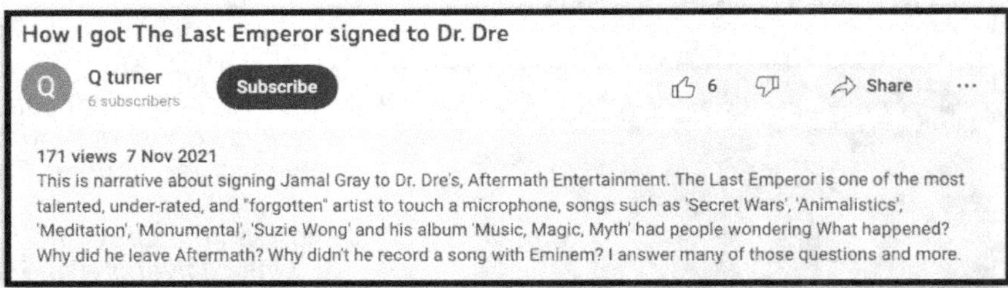

How I got The Last Emperor signed to Dr. Dre

Q turner
6 subscribers

Subscribe

👍 6   👎   ↗ Share   ⋯

171 views 7 Nov 2021
This is narrative about signing Jamal Gray to Dr. Dre's, Aftermath Entertainment. The Last Emperor is one of the most talented, under-rated, and "forgotten" artist to touch a microphone, songs such as 'Secret Wars', 'Animalistics', 'Meditation', 'Monumental', 'Suzie Wong' and his album 'Music, Magic, Myth' had people wondering What happened? Why did he leave Aftermath? Why didn't he record a song with Eminem? I answer many of those questions and more.

think they were part of like the Dungeon Family… You had of course Death Row… So these were the type of labels that they were putting artists on, because at this point, Interscope was seen as a distributor. They weren't putting out the quote on quote 'urban' music. So that put us in a quandry and it took us some time to get off the label. But at the same time, we knew that it was necessary if we wanted to at least have our music see the light of day. We had done some music with Muggs and contractually, Dre was supposed to have the first single. He was going to be the one to introduce us to the world. But again, he was taking relatively long, and Muggs had given us some fire. So if you look at the song that Last Emperor composed, called 'Susie Wong', that was straight for the market. DJ Muggs was Cypress Hill, DJ Muggs was 'Jump Around' for House of Pain… So he had the sound, we now had not just the sound, but we had an audience. So we didn't understand why we couldn't put out some music. We put out the white label which was 'Secret Wars,' so we were making a name for ourselves.

So we got off Aftermath, we desired to be off Aftermath, because Dre was just taking far too long to put out our product. That's our 'why.'

MOST HEADS KNOW the Last Emperor as a hungry wordsmith who patrolled New York and Philadelphia's underground scene in the mid-'90s with an astounding command of the English language, a debonair flow and self-made tracks that left heads processing what he said days after a show.

"What a beautiful world this would be/if you come and spread this black magic with me" went one chorus, and before long, backpackers joined in unison. Since that time, a label deal, a single, a national tour and a forthcoming album have elevated this emcee to supreme, subterranean rapper status.

A recent Interscope Records signee, the Last Emperor describes his outstanding lyrical flow as "descriptive."

"My ability for fine detail and description is what is winning for me right now," he remarks, self-assured.

Fine detail describes his "Secret Wars." This underground anthem began as a crowd teaser and cleverly utilizes every language tool imaginable. From metaphor to allegory, Last Emperor gets loose over an engaging piano-riddled track produced by Mad Soul. An emcee metamorphosis takes place as the Emperor transforms his vocals into a battle between several notable emcees and various comic-book characters.

"Set it off/It's the fight of the century/KRS and Professor X will battle each other mentally, with rhymes/these two team captains waste no time/Charles Xavier tried to invade Kris Parker's mind/he shot a cerebral probe at Kris' mind but he missed it/Professor X taken out by the Blast Master's metaphysics/round two—new fight, word to life, you gotta see this/block the Mortal Combat It's Doc Strange and the Genius/yeah son, he's no match/Let that graphic wizard have it/my liquid swords slashes straight through Doctor Strange's magic."

While the Last Emperor maintains a distinct post in the underground, his spot on 1998's Lyricist Lounge tour made him a household Hip-Hop name across the country.

"It was the ultimate learning experience in terms of tightening up my stage show," the Last Emperor declares. "I learned so much opening for acts like De La Soul and KRS-One" (He combined with the latter and Zack De La Rocha on "C.I.A.," a cut from last year's Lyricist Lounge compilation album).

Although a bit nervous, the Last Emperor found the Lounge audience to be surprisingly embracing throughout the U.S. "As far as Cali was concerned, I was a little weary at first. But because it was an ill tour, people automatically knew what sort of music they were in store for," he explains.

Nevertheless, the tour has come to an end, and in the studio is the place to find the Last Emperor.

"My album is going to be very descriptive," he says. "I already

have a set vision in place that I want to proceed with." The Emperor, at ease in his domain, lays back in Platinum Island Studios where he is currently working a bass-fueled track produced by Shawn J. Period (Mos Def, Artifacts, Heltah Skeltah).

While other album producers and guest appearances are still pending, the Last Emperor has confirmed Prince Paul as executive producer.

With half a dozen songs ready, including "Secret Wars," "Monumental," a confrontational battle rhyme coupled with a mellow, sci-fi-sounding track, and "Bums," whose intricately woven lyrics dominate a slow, funk-influenced, syncopated instrumental already out on wax, the Last Emperor is preparing to conquer them all.

MINAMINA GOODSONG [2000-2006]

Minamina Goodsong! New find worthy of putting others onto. From Smyrna / Atlanta, GA. These cats were pretty active in the early 2000s, releasing four group albums from 2001 to 2005. Their album *The Transcendental Game of Zen* (2003) was recently uploaded to YouTube and is a serious gem. The below artwork should indicate some of the sound you'll hear - but it's along the lines of like a **Mars III** or **Heiruspecs**. Conscious, yet not so religious (at least not overtly). Slightly upbeat and fun (yet not overtly - à la **Ugly Duckling**) and culturally authentic.

The crew consists of members **Adahma AD** (emcee), **Pgnut** (emcee / producer), **Twain** [emcee], and **DJ T'Challa** (producer / DJ). According to their LastFM profile, the group began in 2000 and disbanded in 2006 'after a series of four albums and tours across the country.'

I'm not sure why these cats never got the hype. But there's some serious good ish to be found within the catalogue - even just from a surface exploration. From mentions, Minamina Goodsong appear to be from a crew called '**The Kaleidoscope Crew**' I haven't been able to find any further information on the collective, but if you happen to know more, I'd love to learn.

A.D. of the group began working with producer **Squishy Nice** as '**Squishy Nice and A.D.**'. The two had an album and a 12" out, but also - appeared on the **Syntax Records** compilation *Night Owls 3: The Chiropractor's Goldmine* [2007]. The track featured, called 'Lifetime' is readily available on the interwebs and is utterly fantastic. If I had to pick a favourite out of everything I've heard from Minamina Goodsong, it would be this A.D. solo cut.

Dope rap music here. I have a feeling that Atlanta in general was pretty overlooked in terms of the indie rap space - with many heads associating the region with early trap or party music.

Minamina Goodsong
The Transcendental Game of Zen

Pynut The Prehistoric as
JEBEDIAH NEPTUNE
Tedjon as
BINGO PAJAMA
Adahama Ad as
BARNUM HARBUCK
dj T challa as
TONY CAMARIO

DOO DOO BROWN - FANTASTIC PLANET [1997]

The Urban Emporium uploaded to YouTube a couple weeks back an album from 1991. It was *Ya Rollin' Doo Doo!* by **Doo Doo Brown's** group **2 Hyped Brothers and a Dog.** Miami Bass stuff, not all that interesting, but fun in its novelty to some degree. The peak? was a summertime anthem for college fraternities and sororities, which wasn't good, but it was a good laugh. That said, I was interested to see what else Doo Doo Brown put out - and really more about this cat overall.

I think most know Doo Doo for his role as a comedian over the past decades. From Jacksonville and later Atlanta, he's appeared in some movies, some comedy specials, and even had a run with **Def Jam Comedy** during the 2 Hyped Brothers era. But it turns out, he did put out something after 2 Hyped Brothers. He put out a solo record in 97' called *Fantastic Planet*. And the verdict? From what I gather, it's pretty dope!

Okay, I haven't tracked down the whole thing. But songs do exist on YouTube. This record is night and day different than the Miami Bass sounds of The Hyped Brothers. The record features members of the crew 'Fantastic Planet Players.' As the insert shows, the crew includes: Doo Doo Brown, **Odd-1**, **Mrs**. **Gussie**, **Kromium**, **Sky Eli**, **D.J. Technic**, **Double Vision**, **LowLife** and **Spice**. Discogs classifies it as 'g-funk' and RnB/ Swing. It's darker, more street, more raw. The song *Tell The Truth* includes Mrs. Gussie and Odd-1 along with our front man Doo Doo Brown. Given the 'R&B / Swing' tag, you may have expected the woman in the group to be a singer, but no. Mrs. Gussie shows here that she can rap! But hold up, Gussie isn't the star of this track... There's an **3-Stacks** clone that sounds just *illllll*. It's a little bit darker than Andre 3000 - but with the same flow and cadence. I'm not sure who is who - but the whole thing honestly gives off a **Dungeon Family** or maybe a **Geto Boys** vibe.

Players Makin Geez is less dark. More laid back, more chill, with a smooth R&B hook and rough rhymes. Although I'm not sure who's rapping here, one of the cats has that

grizzly "Watcha Want **Nine**!" voice. This is a dope cut too. Slightly funky, playing off the Fantastic Planet theme, but hard. There's no trace of the Hyped Brothers - and no comedy.

If you manage to find a copy of this, pick it up. It's bound to be worth it at a reasonable price. If you have one to sell, hit me up.

TRAVIS
OUNTY
HRIS
B

Last year I picked up a copy of David Foster Wallace and Mark Costello's **Signifying Rappers.** The two Harvard students were busy writing about a myriad of social issues from their Boston dorm during the late 80s - years before the fame of either writer. In Signifying Rappers, the two take on the topic of hip-hop; a still relatively new pop culture sensation come 1989. What's perhaps most interesting for the hip-hop head, is not Wallace's social critiques and analysis, but Costello's ethnography of the local Boston scene in the late 80s.

Boston, being only four hours away from the Bronx by car, has unsurprisingly had a long history with the culture within its districts. Growing up I knew some about the Boston scene. Institutionally, **The Source Magazine** had its roots in Boston, and acts like **Benzino** (and therefore **The Almighty RSO**) stemmed from the city. Additionally, my go-to online-retailer for underground rap (**UGHH**) had also called Boston home. Additionally, artists such as **Guru**, **Edo G and the Bulldogs**, **Mr. Lif**, **7L & Esoteric**, and **Akrobatik** had instilled well-earned respect for the city early on in my hip-hop journey. Like any scene however, the depth of the talent is only observed when you peak beneath the curtains and begin to dive deep. In Signifying Rappers, Costello began to make that reality clear.

In the time since, I've been fascinated with exploring more of Boston's hip-hop scene. For issue 2, I spoke to **T-Max The Novelist**, my first real attempt to learn and expose myself to the Boston underground scene. Groups like **Concrete Click**, **Wiseguys**, etc. were all present and notable in that story. In the time since T-Max in the 90s, everyone from **Reks**, **Virtuoso**, **Special Teamz** (**Slaine**, Edo G. & **Jaysaun**), **Terminology**, **M-Dot**, and others have made their impact on the scene. In recent years, a new set of voices have arisen from the Boston underground that are certainly worthy of attention: **HRIS**.

HRIS, or History Repeats Itself, actually dates back to the late 90s. However, the recent output of artists like **Bugsy H.**, **S18**, **Matticz** and newcomer **Nonchalantly Zay** are certainly what has put HRIS on the map. My introduction came last year. At the tail end of 2022, Bugsy H., S18 and producer **Masta Conga** put out *Museum of Chryme Art.* The 13 song LP introduced both Bugsy and S18 to my ears. In the months following, Bugsy particularly has made a strong impression. In 2023, he dropped *IFC Classics*, with **LordWillin**, as well as *Travis County 3* with **DJ Kesti**, the latter of which became an instant favourite. The dark, almost horror core-esque style is something rarely charted in 2023. Even more rare, is to see these themes pulled off. (**Esham's** two 2023 releases... why?) Bugsy however, has done just that - with the most recent string of releases proving the emcee a formidable foe in the underground rap landscape, reaching far outside of the streets of Boston.

This piece began with an interview with HRIS-founder Bugsy back at the end of May. What began as simply a conversation with Bugsy, ended in multiple interviews with the current emcee-roster of the HRIS brand. These conversations have not only provided context to the movement, but has introduced me to a scope of new art, some of which has truly blown me away. The most recent album from Nonchalantly Zay, *El Corazon De Oro* received a perfect rating in these pages and is undoubtably one of my favourite albums for the month of July.

I would like to thank Bugsy, S18, Matticz and Zay for taking the time out of their lives to tell their story. For those unaware of the HRIS movement, I hope this piece will encourage you to do some homework. There's a lot of dope rap out there, much of which unfortunately gets casted to the side. Let's not allow that to happen here.

WHAT IS HRIS

The current roster of HRIS includes emcees: Bugsy H., S18., Matticz., and Nonchalantly Zay as well as producers; **Killer Krates**, DJ Kesti, **Isaac No Beats**, **KT** and **Maestro Z**. However, this roster has experienced dramatic change over the years; with artists circulating in and out and the unfortunate passing of key figures.

The earliest rendition of HRIS begins with the duo **The Savage Brothers** in the late 1990s. Not to be confused with the **Snowgoons**-affiliated group from South Carolina, Savage Brothers consisted of Bugsy (likely going by Moonman at the time,) and rhyme partner **Kage**. Although no recorded material surfaced until 2003 - the fascination with darker and horror themed music certainly begins here. In an interview with Bugsy, he explained to me that early records from **Necro** and **Non-Phixion** were staples in his musical journey, with the street raps of **Pun** and **Big L** being significant influences early on.

Kage and Bugsy grew up in the South end of Boston. As noted, Boston was primed for underground and culturally authentic rap. Sure, the mainstream material had it's outlets (Jam'N 94.5) - but those who identified with hip-hop culturally, weren't interested in that. Instead, shows like *At Night* on WERS's 88.9 FM were staples in the Boston scene - and both Bugsy and Kage were active listeners.

Bugsy: *When I was a kid WERS 88.9 FM radio was one of the biggest and most respected underground hip hop shows in the city. Remembered waiting around all day to hear **Masta Ace** come up there and rap.* - interview with **Grégoire Zasa** for **Regulate**.

THE BOSTON GLOBE • SATURDAY, MARCH 7, 1998

Marlon Orozco (left), a manager at the Computer Museum's Computer Clubhouse, talking with member Steve Osemwenkhae.

Upgrading internal drive

By Hiawatha Bray
GLOBE STAFF

Computer Clubhouses help low-income youths develop valuable skills

VLADIMIR SMITH, AGE 14, sat before an Apple Macintosh computer at the Boston Computer Museum's Computer Clubhouse, and turned himself into a monster.

Actually, it was a picture of himself lunging forward with a theatrical snarl on his face. Smith used a computer program to "morph" the image, seamlessly transforming it into a picture of a horned, saber-toothed demon. Smith was proud of his work; it had taken him a couple of hours to get it right. "This program takes a *lot* of time," he said.

Chris Conley, 15, was impressed, but he thought the effect happened too slowly. "You know what you should do?" Conley said. "You should go to where you set the speed, and set it to one second. That's how they do it on TV."

Indeed, Conley and Smith can work with many of the same software tools used by TV special effects wizards, artists and musicians. And they can do it because of an innovative program dreamed up by an MIT professor and Boston's Computer Museum.

The Computer Clubhouse program gives children and teenagers from low-income families a chance to develop valuable computer skills. The first Clubhouse, located next door to the Computer Museum, has been so successful there are now three more in Boston, with a fourth set to open in Dorchester this month. Clubhouses have also opened or are being developed in Brooklyn, N.Y., Columbus, Ohio, and Stuttgart.

Membership in the Clubhouses is free, thanks to financial support from foundations and corporations. The original Clubhouse now has about 150 members, aged 10 to 18.

As people become obsessed with computers and the Internet, the success of the Clubhouses might come as no surprise. What's unexpected is their approach to computer education. There are no teachers here, no lectures, no limits on what the kids can do with the machines.

"We don't do basic training," said Clubhouse director Gail Breslow. Instead, children just sit down and get busy. They're told not to worry about pressing the wrong button. "There's very little they can do to mess it up forever," says Breslow. So much of the learning comes through trial and error. Gradually, children learn how to use a variety of software tools to design artworks, compose music, or create short videos.

One thing you won't find are children playing Tomb Raider or Myst. "It's not a place for youth to go to play games. It's not even a place to go and learn some basic skills on the computer," said Mitchel Resnick, the MIT Media Lab professor who helped create the Clubhouses. "It's more a place for youth to go to create things on these computers."

COMPUTER CLUBHOUSE, Page F2

88.9 FM at Night - mon-fri. 8PM-11PM Weekday evenings get the night rolling with 88.9 FM at night, spinning the latest hip hop tracks from the underground. Listen in for the real deal 5 times a week, straight from the source, 88.9FM.

Monday Night Raw: Optimus

Tape Deck Tuesday: False 1

Way Back Wednesday: Nomadik, Mation

True School Thursday: Diablo

Uh-oh Fridays: Mr. Treze, EQ

Mr. Treze and Optimus

Rob Hunter and Optimus

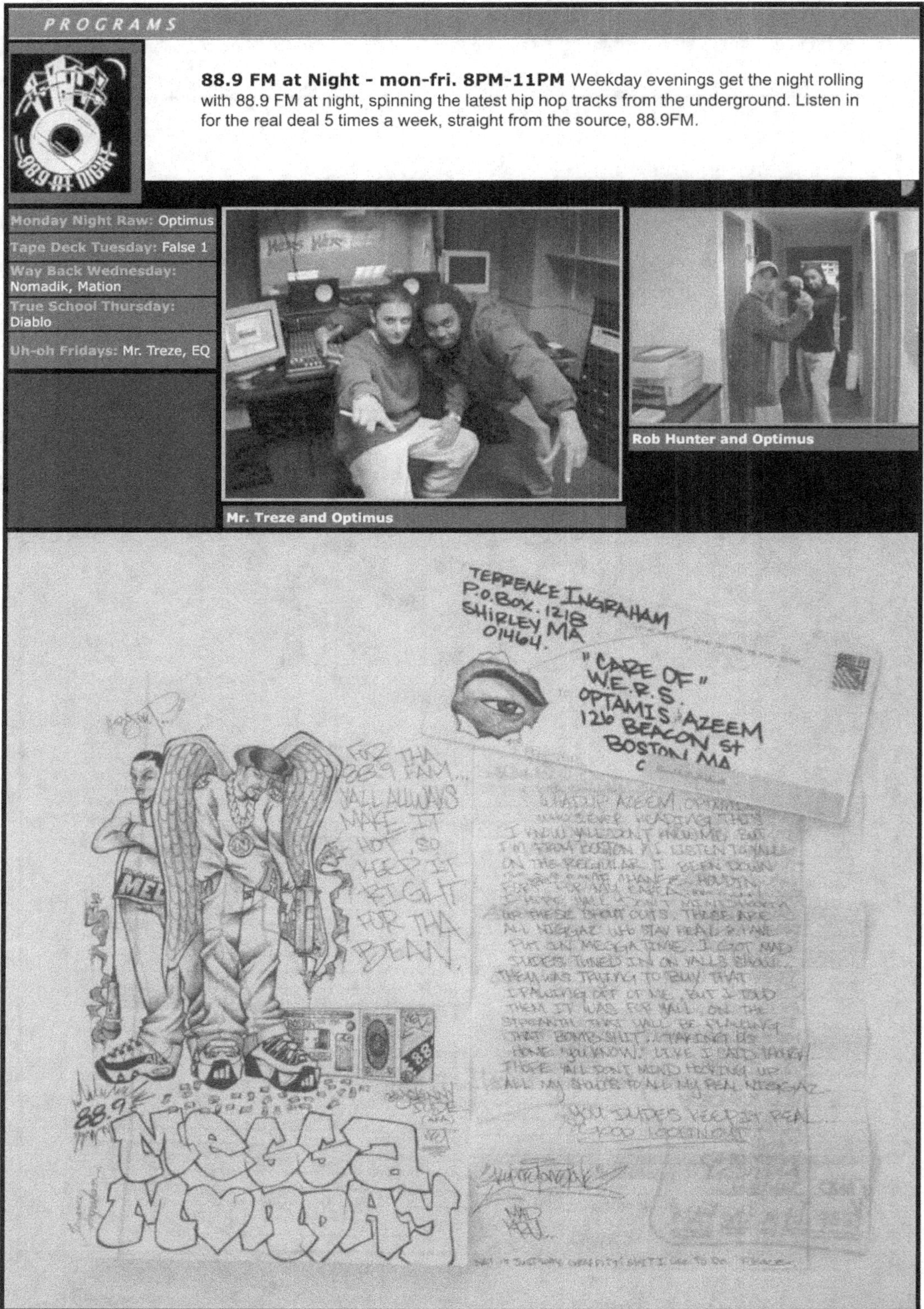

As fans of underground rap, The Savage Brothers duo would record and create mixtapes through a dual cassette deck. These recordings, although influential in their own progress, never saw the light of day. From conversations, artists like Necro were large inspirations, and it's likely that the music shared some similarities with the Brooklyn emcee. Tough, rugged, raw, mean, and dark. In many ways, the same ingredients that make up the HRIS sound today.

In the early 2000s - with The Savage Brothers expanding their own circle, the duo came in need of a group or collective identity. After meeting a local talent by the name '**O**,' the desire to have unity beyond the duo was clear. This was the birth of HRIS, or 'The Hewitt Family,' named after the film *The Texas Chainsaw Massacre*.

Kage and O, like Bugsy, grew up immersed in the Boston street life. And although they were dedicated to their craft, their rhymes alone were not enough to keep them out of trouble. Circulating in and out of Juvenile Detention centres, when the big break for recording time came in 2003, only Bugsy was present.

In 2003, circumstances changed. Boston's **Computer Museum** (later the Museum of Science), had begun offering studio time to youth in the Boston area as part of their '**Clubhouse Program**.' Although the initiative began ten years prior in 1993 as a way to familiarize youth with new technology, by 2003 it had developed into a fully functional recording studio. Engineered by **Square Route**, a local Boston producer, Bugsy invited down to record and utilize the Museum's equipment. This was the first time that Bugsy had access to professional equipment.

> **Bugsy**: *At the time, I was a senior. I was 18 years old and I met my mentor, his name was Square Route, and he used to record these songs… He had this little independent label and they used to record at this studio which was called The Clubhouse. It was the studio in the Museum of Science. So a friend of mine from the block I grew up on, his name was Session, he brought me down there one day and he introduced me to Square Route. Then we started recording what I would say was my first actual recording sessions.*

Describing Square Route as a mentor is absolutely correct. Even twenty years later, Square Route's connection and support of the HRIS movement is clear as day. Through thick and thin, this relationship sustained. In addition to being a direct mentor of Bugsy and fam, Square Route also owned **Math Line Records**. Those studio sessions in 2003 resulted in the album *The Meaning of H.*, released on Math Line and sold independently, hand-to-hand throughout the Boston area. "We used to just sell it out of cars, we would do little venues and sell them at the venues, merch and stuff like that. It wasn't a big album. It wasn't in any stores or platforms or anything. We were really just selling the CD at the time.." Shortly after *The Meaning of H*, the original *Travis County* was recorded and released, also through Math Line Records. These records are near impossible to track down online, but would have featured some of the earliest Bugsy recordings we have.

Around this time, Matticz joined the fold and became inducted into the HRIS family. For all intents and purposes, Matticz is the last member of the original HRIS roster.

> **Matticz:** *I [stepped into the local scene] in like 2003-4 ish. That's when I started recording. That's when I met Bugsy. I went to highschool with him. He took me to the studio with him, it was like a free studio for teenagers to record. I actually started recording there for a long period of time. Either with myself, or bringing other people.*

FOX RACING

For a small run in the mid 2000s, HRIS had some buzz in the local Boston scene. As the crew did shows, performed at open mics, rocked freestyles and the like, the scene around them began to take notice. WELS was playing their records and the group was in talks with Sony Records, a deal that ultimately never panned through. Although the activity in the local scene, and overall lack of recorded material exists during these early years. Finding HRIS material online from 2003-2016 is difficult to say the least. Lives progressed, motivations changed, and frustrations with the music business are certainly factors the careers of many independent artists; HRIS saw no exception.

In 2015, Kage, founding member of the crew - and half of the Savage Brothers, passed away. In many ways, the death of Kage marked a new chapter of the HRIS brand and identity. Future records are made in his honour, and the output has increased tenfold. Rappers S18 and most recently Nonchalantly Zay have been added to round out the lyrical talent of the group, and HRIS has began expanding globally, working with producers from all corners of the globe.

This ramping of motivation is timely. As 2015 transitioned HRIS into new focus, the underground hip-hop landscape was certainly amidst its own change. Army of the Pharaohs, Snowgoons and other dominant forces in the hardcore, underground scene were slowly being replaced by the likes of **Griselda**, **Trust**, **Da Cloth**, **The Umbrella**, and the like. With a new cast of characters, business models also underwent substantial changes. As physical product became more prioritized, albums got shorter and the quantity of releases surged. Furthermore, overseas production has only continued its presence in underground rap. All of this, HRIS has taken advantage of. Like many artists have, HRIS has adapted and found success within the current model.

*To give a scope on the impact of HRIS in recent years, members have collaborated extensively with artists like **Eto**, **M-Dot**, **Aida**, **Tone Spliff**, **Meph Luciano**, **Ca$ablanca**, **M.I.C. Murphy**, **Sypooda**, **Solomon Child**, **Chyna Streetz**, **Slime One**, and others. If you aren't paying attention to HRIS. Tap in.*

THE RECORDS

Although this is not even close to an exhaustive list of the recorded material that HRIS has to offer, the below records represent some of my favourite and noteworthy releases in the catalogue. My aim is to give is a sense of what HRIS has to offer and to highlight particular gems. I believe these thirteen will do that. This is in no particular order.

---

1. Nonchalantly Zay - El Corazon De Oro [2023]

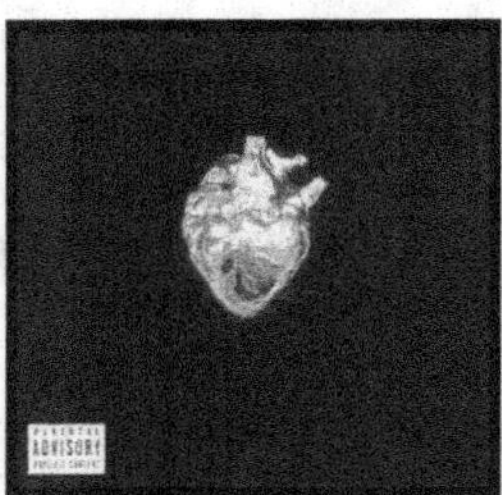

Let's begin with my favourite record from HRIS thus far. If you have to listen to anything to understand the potential of the crew - this is it. 'Children of the Corner,' 'Hard Timez,' and 'Sol-id' with guest verses from Postman L & J-Hot are just three of my favourites. Great hooks, fantastic beat selection, and a voice you will remember on the mic. Some of the best street rap you'll find in 2023.

2. DJ Kesti x DirtyDef - Beat Tapes 1-4 [2023]

Incredible work by Kesti and DirtyDef here and what a way to start off 2023. I'm not too familiar with DirtyDef, however HRIS's DJ Kesti is a French producer hailing from the city of Amiens. Over the past few months four of these have dropped in total, and each one sees the two trading beats back and forth. Creatively crafted hard bangers. From the wonkier 'Canon Scié' to the piercing 'Blizzard Chase.' And those are just Kesti's first two tracks! Great beats, amazing series.

3. Bugsy H. x Mindframe - Sanctuary [2021]

*This is one of the earlier Bugsy releases I've heard, and one of the few things I've heard produced by Mindframe. Eto kicks it off with the first verse and **sheeesh.** Don't you just love Eto? Dark piano loops with heavy rhymes. 'Who Would Ever Think,' is another stand out, with a more playful aesthetic despite the grimier undertones of the subject matter. Quite a long album - but worth the investment. A lot to love here.*

4. S-18 - Bronze Edition [2023]

S18 grew up listening to the Wu-Affiliates like Sunz of Man and Killarmy. That sound is alive and well on this LP. Hell, we even get a Solomon Childs feature near the end. The album is called 'The Bronze Edition,' and coincidentally enough, it sounds like something that Bronze Nazareth would be putting out during this leg of his career. My favourite shit is the play on the nursery rhyme, with 'Wheels on the Barrel.' Solid joint right here.

5. Bugsy H. & DJ Kesti - Travis County 2 [2019]

It's been a few years since Travis County 2 was released, and you can clearly see growth in the emcee from project to project. Although Bugsy is arguably at a more primitive state on Travis County 2, it in no way means that the album is deprived of quality. Kesti is seriously a top tier producer in the lane that he occupies and should be more sought after for beats. This shit is grimy and creatively unique. Check it.

6. Nonchalantly Zay x The Beatenaunt - The Foreigners [2022]

Nonchalantly Zay produced by The Beatenaunt. A presentation of Boston, "coming straight from the slums" of the South End. Way more soulful and laid back than 'El Corazon De Oro,' and a bit more hollowed out. A very strong deliverance, even if not quite as memorable as my first introduction with El Corazon. Favourite track ought to be 'Word Play' with JFliz and Tone Spliff. Marching forward beat by beat, that shit is ill.

7. Maestro Z - The Cookout Vol. 1 [2023]

A large an expansive, 25 track beat tape from the one and only Maestro Z. Each song, co-produced by another beatsmith. There's a lot to love here. With skits and interludes throughout, this thing feels more like an instrumental album than a beat tape, and good for it. 'Night Contra' is a favourite. Some soulful sounds at times, in the vein of perhaps a Wavy Da God, but identifiably hard and gutter. Rapper's take note!

8. Bugsy H. & DJ Kesti - Travis County 3 [2023]

Brutal, dark and hard. This is what you can expect with Bugsy through and through. That said, this album stands out. Despite over twenty years in the game, Bugsy is still improving with each release. Perhaps too is DJ Kesti, as these beats are strong. This album features Eto, Lungs, Black Prince, among others. The Eto featured, 'Lee Smith,' is easily a favourite along with 'Artifacts' with Stephen Route.

9. The 88 Marksmen - Museum of Crhyme Art [2022]

This was the first album from HRIS that I had heard late last year, after only hearing members on features and production credits prior. Super hard, dark, boom bap, grimy rap. Even the way the tape starts off with 'Hardly Hiring Staff Now,' you know exactly what you're going to get. Just bangers. This one is really dope. Bugsy H., S18 and Masta Conga make up The 88 Marksmen. The highlights off here are A+ material. Don't sleep.

10. Bugsy H. x LordWillin - IFC Classics [2023]

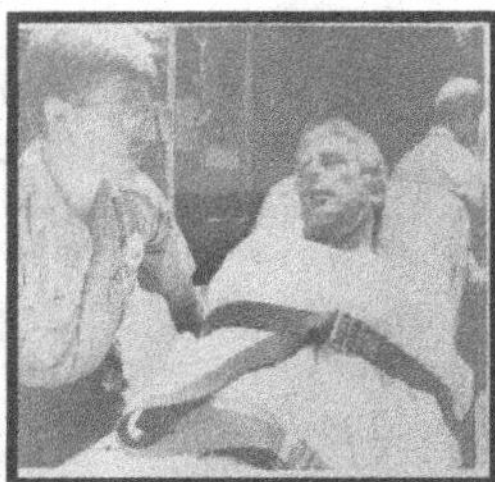

Stokable to see Bugsy collaborate with LordWillin, a long time favourite from his appearance on Snowgoons 'Kraftwerk' in 2010. He used to be pretty active, did some stuff with Slaine, Pryme Prolifik, etc. And recently has done a lot with Lord Rome. This thing is worth it for 'A Life Full of Sins,' alone, storytelling in style. Lots of gems to be found on this tape and strong vibes overall. Solid.

11. Bugsy H. x Wolfman Jeckyll - Night Terrors [2023]

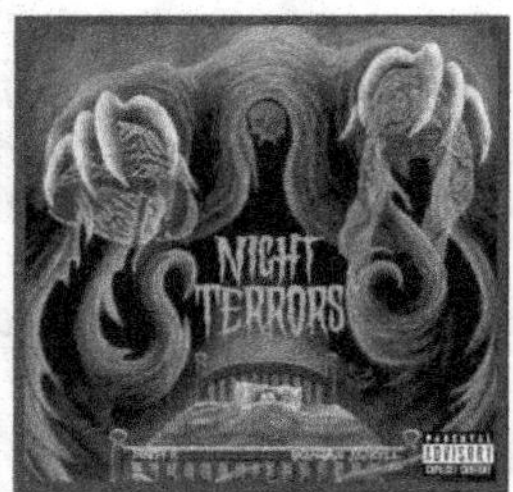

Described as a trip through the 'dream world,' and into the 'subconscious realm.' Masterfully produced by Wolfman Jeckyll with the two trading verses. Moments like the Caribbean-styled hook on 'Nightfall' stand out, but are always just as infectious as the rest. This might be my favourite Bugsy joint to date. The pounding drums on 'Ride This Ride…' literally everything off this album is dope. Check it. What a joint.

12. Matticz - No Love 4 Tha Opps Vol. 1 [2020]

The last of the OG members of HRIS. Matticz has less material out than most of the others, however Spotify does have No Love 4 Tha Opps readily available. Released in 2020, the tape features both Bugsy and Gio Mage on multiple tracks, along with guest spots from Gutter, M Gramz, Dae Toney and Tay. There's some memorable moments off here, like the intro track with Bugsy, 'The Opposition,' but there's also a fair amount of songs that clash with the vibe we've come to expect, such as the more modern-trap influenced 'Throw It Back.'

BONUS: A CLOSER LOOK AT THE KESTI & DIRTYDEF BEAT TAPES.

My new favourite beat series of 2023 goes to this right here. Trading beats back and forth, this is a flux of creativity within a perceived stale genre of gloomy dark bangers. The same intrigue that Stoupe would spark when listening to *Blood in Blood Out* or *A Storm of Swords*. Since the quality is worth blabbing on about, and since I listened to these anyway, why not provide a bit of a deeper look. These are available on Bandcamp for free download or donation. Hopefully we'll see some tapes in the future. Each tape is roughly 20 minutes.

1. *This thing is one hell of a beat tape. Every single beat on this thing is exciting. Rarely do you see a tape within the grimier pockets of the underground sustain such consist interest and enjoyment. It's hard to even pick highlights… Kesti draws comparisons with Stoupe or Giallo Point, with these really wild and creative ideas. DirtyDef feels a bit more cinematic and atmospheric. Everything off of here works. These cats should be bigger than they are.*

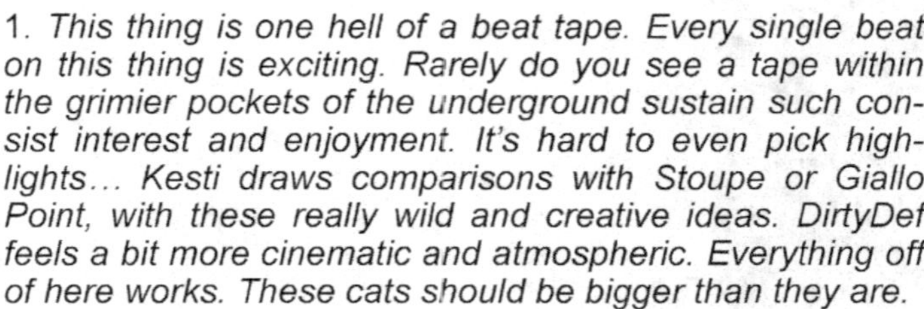

2. ***What a cool turn!*** *Going into #2, I simply wanted more of #1. However, the second instalment takes a shift. It's more hallowed out, more eerie, and shows an entirely new side of both producers. DirtyDef shines here with the two matching styles. A very different vibe - but not a decrease in quality by any stretch. No stoppage of creativity either. Kesti's QHS flares like Stargate Command on lock-down. Def's 'Bullet Proof' brings crime to the Cheers set. A++.*

3. *I dig how they alternate who goes first. It's a small attention to detail, but since these are individually and cohesively themed, it's fun to see who kicks starts the direction at the beginning of each tape. Although there are some real high moments on this thing (DirtyDef's Contamination is just disgusting!), I will say #3 is probably my least favourite of the series. That said, this is in no way a bad tape. It's a little more stale at times, but you can vibe to these heavy even in its weakest moments.*

4. *Back to Kesti kicking it off here. 'Smiling Face' from DirtyDef is well worth the price of admission alone. I could see 38 Spesh rocking this heavy. Actually… It sounds like it belongs among Necro's beats for The Godfather's album with G-Rap. How dope. This thing is just as wild and eccentric as the first. 1+2 share an energy - a vibrancy. There's gloomy dark, and there's combat-attack dark, and this is the latter. Really ill beats to catch me up to the series. Insane run.*

VAULTED:

INTERVIEWS FROM THE VAULT.

DATE: JULY 19 2020
WHO: CELPH TITLED
ORIGINALLY FOR: YOUTUBE (TUV)

TUV: Welcome to The Underground Vault. My name is Alex, I have here with me, one of my absolute favourite emcees. From Equilibrium, to the Demigodz, to Army of the Pharaohs to the thousand fucking features... Please welcome... Celph... Motherfucking... Titled. What's good my man?

CT: Yessir! What's good man? It's been a minute man. We did one of these a long time ago.

TUV: We've definitely spoken before. I know we haven't done an actual interview. But we definitely spoke. When I was running TheUndergroundVault.ca at that period of time, maybe 2013-2014 - whenever Apathy's Connecticut Casual album ended up coming out, we did a small little ad campaign through there.

CT: Yup.

TUV: I think that was probably the last time I talked to you? Or wait, I hit you up about a compilation the *Black Sunz Compilation* at some point as well. The one that Anonymous Twist ended up putting together. So we've talked.

CT: First interview, yeah. But I've been down with The Underground Vault for a minute.

TUV: I wanted to talk about history and to go through your career in as much detail as I really can. Because I think for a lot of people - I know yourself, you don't do a

mid 80s maybe, and they had like the boom box and they had finished the lawn waiting for the dude and they had like a boom box playing, had put down the cardboard and were doing all the breakdancing. I had never seen nothing like that before. So that was really my first hip-hop memory, I guess. I recognized it as something new.

But I wasn't really into the dancing or anything. I had just liked the beat. From there, any time I caught it. MTV would start to play rap songs here and there... **Yo! MTV Raps** was pretty early on MTV. They were around in 1988 or so, at least. But I never really got into the graff... I'm just a music guy. The music always drew me in. I was never really compelled to... I mean, I respected the graffiti and respected the b-boying and all that. And still do, but just some people gravitate towards that, and others gravitate towards the music.

whole lot of interviews. Some press interviews from time to time, but you don't do a lot of interviews. And as a fan myself, there's been a lot of things that I wanted to talk about.

I wanted to start before Equilibrium and your early roots in the culture. We all know you as a rapper, and I think most people that follow you know your production catalogue as well, at least to some degree - but what incited you to get into the culture? And was there ever an interest in other elements, like graffiti, or dance during those early years?

CT: I mean, the first like hip-hop memory I have is growing up down here in Florida. It's different than growing up in New York or Philly or LA or something in terms of being exposed to hip-hop just everywhere you go. Even back then. But really? I think I remembered my grandfather had hired some dudes to do his lawn and they were from Puerto-Rico I think. Puerto-Rico from New York. This was like the

But I really didn't rap. I wasn't into rapping in the beginning. I was into making beats. So the first beats I made were really just like Miami Bass style. Like booty-shake beats. Cause that's what was poppin' down here. A lot of my early hip-hop was stuff like that. **Like 2 Live Crew, DJ Magic Mike** from Orlando... All that bass type music. So that was my first. In terms of making hip-hop? It was that type of stuff. Then later I got into trying to rap. So that's the beginning.

TUV: Equipment wise, what were you using at that period of time? Cause equipment is expensive, especially as a kid in the early 90s. An MPC, or an SP1200 is expensive. Were you just making pause tapes in your room?

CT: Nah. My Dad had access. He worked for a trucking company back in the 80s or whatever. So he had access to new technology stuff, pretty cheap or whatever. So we had a PC real early on. Like a home computer in the

80s. So we had this old computer and it had a modem and you used to be able to call. This was really before the internet, so you could dial a local bulletin board system. It was somebody else's computer, it was called a BBS. I don't know if you've ever heard anything like that, but this is like pre-AOL, pre-internet, everything.

But you could like connect to somebody else's computer through the phone, and they had files. And I eventually found a composing program, it was called Mod-Edit. That's the name of the program, and you could track music in it. And a lot of people used it. There was like different scenes in that realm at the time. A lot of people from Europe used this program or whatever, but they would make like dance tracks. It was made to make dance music.

I just started messing with that. So I started making beats on like an old computer. Like an old PC computer. With that program. This was a time when… this was before Windows. This computer ran an operating system called MS-Dos. So this is like really early. So I started making beats on that equipment right there.

TUV: So ModEdit, was that software specifically made for dance music? Or was that simply the community that latched onto it? Cause if you're doing like the Miami Bass shit, it's high BPM, it kind of goes hand in hand I would imagine?

CT: Yeah. Well, the tempo is really the only difference with Miami Bass and dance music or whatever. My point is, I didn't really know anyone making hip-hop. I was the only person I knew who made hip-hop or even Miami Bass beats on it. Everyone else I heard was making like house music on it. But there might have been other people. I'm not saying I'm the first one to make hip-hop beats on it, but I didn't know anyone else who did that or used it for that.

TUV: The Tampa thing is really interesting. So I don't know about much about Tampa hip-hop history. I know of yourself, and the stuff you end up rocking with. Funkghost a little bit later on… but mostly I know Tampa as a skate scene. The Tampa Am, and the skate culture happening in Tampa. When you were growing up, was there much of a local rap community in the city? You mention the Puerto-Rican guys doing the breakdancing in the mid 80s, was there much of a community in Tampa at the time?

```
        Track 1          Track 2          Track 3          Track 4      Abbreviated Sample List
00 F 2 15 1 02    D 3 07 0 00    C 3 14 0 00    C 3 19 F 02
01 G 2 15 3 0A    ... 00 0 00    ... 00 0 00    ... 00 F 03   01 }}} maf   17
02 ... 00 3 00    ... 00 0 00    ... 00 A 03    ... 00 F 02   02 23 rue d  18
03 ... 00 3 00    ... 00 0 00    ... 00 A 03    ... 00 F 03   03     68720  19
04 ... 00 3 00    ... 00 0 00    ... 00 A 03    ... 00 F 02   04           20
05 ... 00 0 00    ... 00 0 00    ... 00 A 03    ... 00 F 03   05           21
06 ... 00 4 81    D 3 02 0 00    D#3 12 0 00    ... 00 F 02   06    create  22 <<NONE>>
07 ... 00 4 00    ... 00 0 00    ... 00 0 00    ... 00 F 03   07         d  23 <<NONE>>
08 ... 00 4 A2    ... 00 0 00    ... 00 0 00    ... 00 F 02   08           24 <<NONE>>
09 ... 00 4 00    ... 00 0 00    ... 00 0 00    ... 00 F 03   09           25 <<NONE>>
10 ... 00 4 00    D 3 03 0 00    ... 00 0 00    ... 00 F 02   10           26 <<NONE>>
11 ... 00 4 00    ... 00 0 00    ... 00 0 00    ... 00 F 03   11           27 <<NONE>>
12 G#2 15 3 F0    D 3 04 0 00    G 2 14 0 00    ... 00 F 02   12           28 <<NONE>>
13 ... 00 0 00    ... 00 0 00    ... 00 0 00    ... 00 F 03   13           29 <<NONE>>
14 ... 00 0 00    ... 00 0 00    ... 00 A 03    ... 00 F 02   14           30 <<NONE>>
15 ... 00 0 00    ... 00 0 00    ... 00 A 03    ... 00 F 03   15           31 <<NONE>>
                                                              16

Editing pattern 0.
Default sample: 01.
Press 'N' to hear the note the cursor is on.
Press 'P' to hear the entire pattern.

ARTICHOK.MOD: 39 patterns,58 song length,21 samples.  4294326144 bytes free.
```

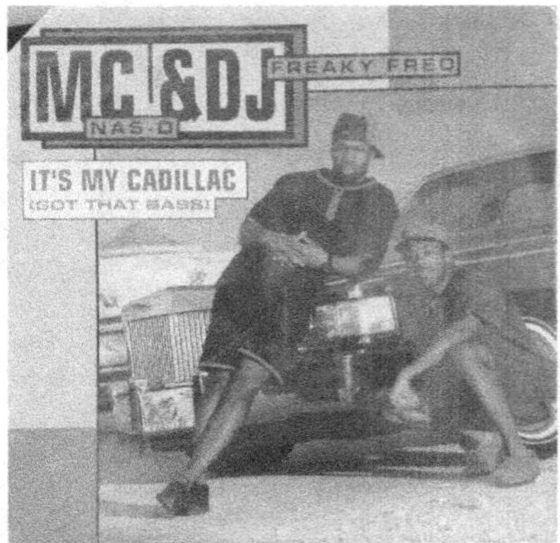

CT: Nah, like that event with the dudes breakdancing, they were from New York. So they were into the real hip-hop type stuff. Down here, as far I know, I didn't know a lot of other rappers. I never seen local people breakdancing and what not. But what was big down here was like I said bass music.

There really hasn't been much of a big scene just cause this city is not really… I can't explain it, but it's not really known for hip-hop. But we do have it here. In the late 80s, early 90s, a lot of people don't know this, but a pivotal guy in Tampa hip-hop was **DJ Kenny K**, rest in peace. But he was a part of **Digital Underground**. And Digital Underground has roots here in Tampa. **Shock G,** I'm not sure if he's from Tampa or whatever, but he lived here. He grew up down here and then moved to Oakland and did the whole Digital Underground thing. But Kenny K was a DJ in Digital Underground but he stayed here and he ran, which was pretty much the only hip-hop show we had it was on the community radio station; **WMNF** 88.5. So he was pretty much the pioneer in terms of like hip-hop roots here. We got a lot of bass booty shake music like I said. We had… the first record I really remember down here, it was like 91-92, it was called '**My Cadillac**,' by this group **MC Nas-D and DJ Freaky Fred**. Like some bass music.

Trying to think… A lot of people don't realize, Tampa is the first… well, not first, but we were one of the first cities to ride around with slowed-down music. Like how **DJ Screw** did in Houston? Except we didn't call it 'screw' we called it, 'slowed-down.' And there was a DJ named **Rocket Rod** who was real renowned in the city. And he had a little record shop and he sold these tapes. It would be like all the latest rap songs slowed down, so that you could ride to it. People like to do it because the system… it really made the bass drag out and rumble. So I don't know how long Houston had been doing their thing, and I'm not going to argue who was first, but I'm pretty sure had been doing it as long as them, dating back to the 80s. They just got the recognition for it by the rest of the world. But that's pretty much it.

I mean, we had a big crew down here called **Jam Pony Express**. Some of the founding members were from Fort Lauderdale and then they connected with some of the guys up here. They were like rocking the parties down here. They put out lots of mixtapes. That's pretty much it. That was the early scene. Like I said, we didn't really have like a lyrical or more traditional east coast scene… it was very ghetto music, bass music, dance music, party music… We're a party city. We invented a lot of dances here. In more recent years they call it 'Juk-City' just cause of the dances… Just a club town.

TampaHipHop.com

v1.0

Home Message Board Music Artists DJ's Events Store Services Kenny-k

— Kenny K —

Biography

In the fall of 1986, WMNF restructured it's programming and the station managers realized they were in dire need of a Rap show. When Kenny Waters, who normally wore suits, walked into their staff meeting sportin' suede Pumas, fat laces, a baseball hat and a gold chain, he promised to be the answer to their problem. He had just recently been turned down by the long-standing urban boss, WTMP and was looking for a radio wave that would broadcast his love for Hip-Hop. The program director, Randy Wynn, said "He seemed to be into the music. He had a good audition tape." And just like that, a local star was born. Kenny immediately went on the air.

By the summer of 1987, anyone who was listening to Hip-Hop knew of Kenny K. People all over the 813 area, which used to cover all of southwest Florida, would gear up, prepare their cassette tapes and tune into 88.5 WMNF every Saturday night at Midnight. Anyone that I've spoken with regarding those Saturday nights recalls excitement wondering what remedy Kenny had planned for the Top 40 blues. While the format of his show did change by the summer of 1987, WMNF listeners never heard what Q105 was playing unless is was incorporated in a "wax attack."

In the beginning, Kenny K spun anything that was Rap, including M.C. A.D.E, Gucci Crew II, KJ and Cooley C. Over time, he shied away from "Miami Bass" artists and strictly directed the Technic 1200s towards New York-based Hip-Hop. The reason for this was not because he had no love for the Miami artists, but because of our location. Kenny K felt that Tampa was so highly exposed to what was going on in Miami that playing 2 Live Crew would have been overkill. What he sought to do was play music that couldn't be heard in the Bay area. Kenny K frequently played artists in the same class as Eric B. & Rakim, Dana Dane, Public Enemy and Kool Moe Dee. Had he not spun these now classics, surely a large amount of Hip-Hop fans in the Bay area would never have even heard them. When "My Melody" by Eric B. & Rakim and "Pump that Bass" by Original Concept dropped, there was no Yo! MTV Raps to broadcast those jams into people's homes. In the 813, there was WMNF and one Kenny K. The highlights of his shows besides Hip-Hop "wax attacks" included featuring local artists like The Dedicated Brothers (who former DJ Domination manager Nick Major was a part of) and guest DJs like Scooby D and The M & M DJs.

Anyone who remembers Kenny's show surely remembers the "K-Ettes." The "K-Ettes" were a flock of B-Girls, who dedicated their free time to Kenny and the WMNF listeners. They would take caller requests, shout outs and even accompany Kenny to local clubs and malls to boost his ratings. The most popular "K-Ette" was Lavida "K" Anderson, sister to NFL star Jamal "Juggy" Anderson. Lavida "K" was often the voice callers would hear when dialing 226-3003 to give their shout outs.

By 1988, Kenny K was married to Lavida, employed by Camelot Records in Tampa Bay Center and working hard with Tampa native, Shock G from the Digital Underground crew. Their underground classic "Underwater Rimes" (T.N.T. Records) was in heavy rotation at the time. Not long after, Kenny took a break from the airwaves, and headed out to Oakland with Shock G to work on Digital Underground's "Sex Packets" album. Digital Underground's September '89 release "Doowutchyalike" featured Kool Kenny on the B-side cut, "Hip-Hop Doll."

He returned to WMNF's airwaves in 1990 and continued to spin the real Hip-Hop until 1991. During this span, he worked with Digital Underground and Chuck D. from Public Enemy.

Kenny "K" Waters, the Brooklyn-born WMNF DJ and Hillsborough High School graduate, blessed the 813 airwaves from 1986 to 1993. His career was stopped short by the need of a liver transplant in late 1993. Kenny "K" Waters died in early February 1994. Due to the fact that he did not have health insurance, his name was not admitted to the waiting list for organ donors. Because of his insurance dilemma, he was turned down by Tampa General Hospital and flown to The University of Texas' John Sealy Hospital. Kenny K's surgery would have cost $250,000. - KRAM ®

:::Kenny K Tapes and CDs:::

The TampaHipHop.Com staff currently has Kenny K. mixshow CDs recorded from 1986 to 1988 for *trade only*. If you have a tape that may be of interest to the staff, please contact us immediately. It is highly possible that a trade can be arranged. You can also post tapes or CDs for trade or sale in the SWAP SHOP forum on TampaHipHop.Com message board.

Audio

The Dedicated Brothers feat. Dazzlin' Doc P. This was recorded live by kramtronix® in January '87! Check out the Cool Breeze beatbox outro!

One of Kenny K's best Mixes! This is SOS Band's "The Finest" mixed over "Show Me" by the Cover Girls!

La-Di-Da-Di Kenny K. Style!!

The Most Requested Kenny-K. Wax Attack Mastermix!

Kenny's Janet Jackson "Control" acapella over Run D.M.C.'s "It's Like That" instrumental. Recorded during the summer of 1987.

Kenny cutting Eddie Murphy.

Kenny K. speaks. 01/21/87
Kenny did a lot of talking on his radio show. During that era, WMNF was not equipped with the then hi-tech equipment to broadcast callers over the air. Three or four of his "K-Ettes" would volunteer their time to man the phones and painstakingly *write down* info that callers would provide for Kenny's "Shout outs" portion of the show. I, as many other listeners surely did, would press the "pause" button during this period and resume once Kenny was done. This is one of the few I actually recorded. Looking back on it now, I wish I would have never "paused." They say hindsight is always 20/20. - KRAM®

Unknown Track (recorded 01/21/87). If someone out there can tell us what this jam is called and who the artist is, we will ship you a *FREE* Kenny K. mix CD from the tampahiphop.com archives.

"Dana Dane With Fame" cut up Kenny K. style.

Alexander O'Neal "Criticize" mixed with Kid 'N Play's "Do This My Way." Recorded during the summer of '87.

1 year before Kenny K. was involved with Digital Underground, Kenny *did* bust an occasional rap on the air, and it went a little something like THIS.

The infamous "Peter Piper" mix, recorded 11/01/86 by Sandman.

"Krs One Live On 88.5", recorded by Sandman. Aug. 13, 1988

RIP Kenny-K

TUV: That Kenny K show that they you're talking about - did they offer the opportunity to call in, have freestyles on air, that kind of thing? Could you just go to the station and chill? How much of a community was that show?

CT: Well, specifically Kenny K is before my time. When he was around, i'm like 8-9-10-11. But when he passed away, a brother by the name of **Mad Links** took the spot. That's pretty much my era where I came in. But same station, same show. But I'm not really familiar with how the Kenny K show was. But Mad Links show? Yeah, he did have a call in. There were regulars that would call in. It was a different vibe than **Stretch and Bobbito**. It was a little more serious. But yeah, we went up there as **Equilibrium**. We went on there early, like 96-97. And Mad Links would give local artists a chance. All ya gotta do is a call them up and say, "yo, I got a demo, we're from Tampa, we wanna come up there." And he'd pretty much make it happen.

TUV: So at what point in time do you begin writing? The first section of your career you're focused more on the production side of things, when do you start writing and practicing to rap?

CT: Umm, probably like 93-94. A lot of the stuff I was into at that time was a lot of Bay Area and west coast shit. I was into a lot of **Spice-1** and **E40**. All that type of stuff. So a lot of my real early stuff I did, it kind of sounded like Bay Area stuff. That's why I had a lot of fun when I did the **Bo$$ Hogg Barbarian$** album with **J-Zone**. Because I was able to do a lot of that Bay Area funk type stuff on there.

So yeah, my early stuff was that. And I wasn't real lyrical, I was just kind of like… funked out. [Laughs]. Then like maybe more towards 95', I started taking it more serious. I wanted to be more ill with it. I was trying to be like really complex. Do all these crazy… really push it. I basically went from one extreme to the other. I was just trying to be like laid-back funk type stuff and then I wanted to be like the illest dude in the world.

TUV: Why bother? Obviously it turned out really well for you - but at the time, why get into rap? Productions going well. If you a bit of a leg up in terms of technology. You have a sound that you're adopting. What pushed you to start writing?

CT: I really didn't know anyone else that rapped like that, at that time. Or wanted to take it serious. So, I had to make the music. I had to produce for myself. So that's pretty much why, because I wanted to make records. I did eventually develop the passion to want to rap, but it started with just making beats.

TUV: A few years ago, Apathy ended up putting out that *Alien Tongue* compilation. Just early demo stuff that he did either with himself, or Eternia… but around like 94 to 97-98, that kind of thing. Is there ever a case where will be able to hear some of this material from you? When you don't have your own style or sound yet but still just experimenting?

CT: It's possible. I mean, I really cringe at those things… but I know fans would like to hear it. Just to hear the progress or hear h i s t o r y . B u t m a y b e n o t . I don't even know if I will go back that far, because really I don't even know if I could find the tapes and the quality of it or whatever… The only thing I'm thinking of doing, and me and the guys have been talking about it with Equilibrium,

is we were supposed to come out with like a full length album in the late 90s or whatever… all of those singles that came out were parts of that, that we never actually put out. So I may do something, we may put that out…

TUV: So when did you actually form Equilibrium, and how did you meet Dutch Massive and Magik Most?

CT: I mean, the funny thing is… and a lot of people may not realize this, but I guess I owe a lot to these dudes **Live Poets** was there

name at the time, and they eventually went on to become **Anticon**. I'm sure you're familiar with them.

TUV: 100% Yeah.

CT: Yeah, so really… back in the day, **Sole** from Live Poets at the time, and **Moodswing 9** of that group, I had connected to them, as I said, when I talked about being early on with like downloading files from like local bulletin board systems, of course when AOL came around and you could use that as a gateway to get on the internet, that's where I really connected with a lot of like-minded, independent hip-hop. People putting out records that knew all about the scene. So that's how I connected with Sole and Moodswing. Sole is actually the one who connected me and **Apathy**. Moodswing is the one who connected me and **Dutch**. That was just, I guess Dutch somehow connected with Moodswing and Moodswing was like, "aye, I know another guy from Tampa, you guys would be dope." So he gave him the number and we connected. And then **Magik Most** was with Dutch. They were a group themselves just the two of them was a duo. I forget the name of the group at the time.

TUV: That's fascinating. Was that the type of music you were listening too at that time? The early Anticon shit? You mention like the West Coast influence with Spice-1 and what not, but the Anticon sound is radically different than that. Right?

CT: Right, yeah no. I really didn't mess with the Anticon thing just in terms of my personal taste wise, I didn't really like when they moved to that style. I'm talking this is before they were Anticon. This is when they were doing traditional hip-hop. Like when they were this group called the Live Poets. So if you listen to that album, it's very traditional boom-bap. Just raw samples and straight up rhyming. It's not really where they tried to go in another direction. Which I totally salute, and I salute their work for them and I'm all for taking you wherever your creativty takes you. But yeah, this is before that. So when it moved into that sound, like I said, I saluted them, but it wasn't really my style.

TUV: Okay, so with Equilibrium then. You talked about wanting to put out the album. Why did it never come out?

CT: I mean, we had some turmoil. We were young, we were kids. We clashed heads. So we kind of broke up for a period of time. Like Magik Most, he wasn't in the group for a while. So it also just disbanded at that point. And shortly after we did that album, I moved to New York and just got wrapped up in all that. Shortly after that we became cool with Magik again, that was just a short little thing

that happened. So we was all good but like I said, I had gotten busy doing other stuff. And at that point I just wanted everyone to start fresh. That's why they did their solo things and I helped them with that as well. So yeah, the album just kind of fizzled out. It was unfinished. If I put it out now, I'm going to have to put it out with what it is… There's parts of it unfinished. Just the direction changed. The focus changed. You look at it as 'old material,' you know what I'm saying? Two years later… I didn't have as much interest in putting it out. I did the best I could, I put out a couple 12"s from it. But that's it. There's only like 4-5-6 songs out there.

TUV: If you do end up putting it out, would it just come out through your own imprint through Dirty Version? Or maybe go with like Chopped Herring or something like that? I know there's a lot of labels interested in those early demos. J-Zone put his early stuff with Bob from Chopped Herring. Would that be something you'd think of? Or would you just do it yourself?

CT: Yeah, no. Something like that? I mean, I know how to put out records pretty well. So I

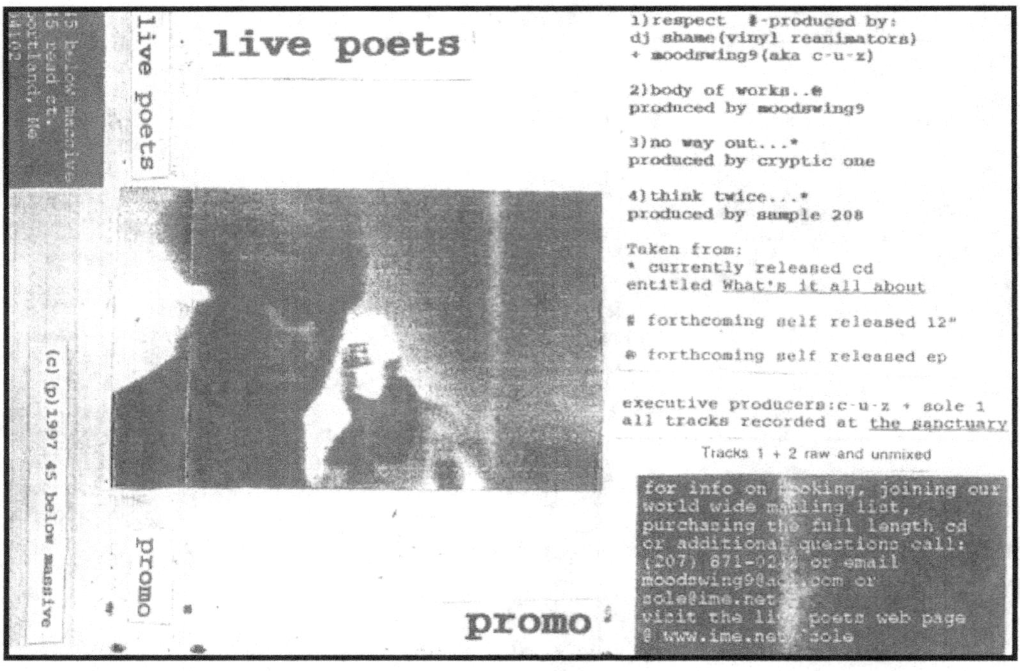

really wouldn't want somebody else taking a cut. I don't know if it'd be **Dirty Version**, it'd probably just be like me, Magik and Dutch would just put it out ourselves on some kind of imprint and you know…

TUV: *The Gatalog*. **When the** *Gatalog* **comes out, it's unprecedented. Four discs. Pretty much all the guest spots you had done up until that period of time. It's missing instrumental cuts and production cuts. But I think most people saw that as your debut. I have two questions: one - what made you put out something of this caliber? And then two: did you anticipate that this was going to be billed as your debut by a lot of cats?**

CT: Ummm, Yeah. Well, really, it started with Apathy when we did the, *It's the Bootleg Muthafuckas Vol. 1.* That was a double-CD compilation of all of his stuff, so I was like, "man, I gotta do one too." But at the time, I had like exploded over the years prior doing so many features. I was just on so many records.

So I was like, "it's gotta be more than a double-CD. So yeah, I just called around like some pressing plants and was like, "yo, is it possible to do a four-disc thing like in a case or whatever?" and they said yeah. So I made it four discs. I knew that it would be unique as no one else had done that.

So it was kind of like a gimmick in a way. Like I knew that it would sell based on that. Even people didn't know who I was or were not that interested in me, but collect hip-hop records might still buy it just because it's unique.

TUV: Yeah plus it was marked down to like a regular CD price. Like I think on UGHH it was selling for like 20-25 bucks?

CT: Yeah pretty much, it wasn't nothing crazy for all those CDs. Yeah. I knew people would call it an album, which I really don't like cause it's just a cluster fuck or so much random shit. It's so random. Then there's stuff on there from when I'm like super young and I sound like totally different… So it's weird. But yeah, it's just a good way to like archive all that shit. Like a compilation where you can just have it all on one set.

But I knew that people would say that it's my album. But it's all good. I mean, people are gonna say what they're gonna say… There's not much you can do.

TUV: Up until that point, you were putting out feature after feature after feature. You were appearing on pretty much any underground rap album and it was pretty diverse. But you hadn't actually put out an album. What was the reason for holding off and not releasing an album from 2000, I guess right till the album with Buckwild in 2010? That's a long period of time, and you put out a lot of work within that period of time, but why no album?

CT: Umm, I mean, I had been working on one. And I still have those records actually, and I will put them out on like a lost tapes kind of thing at one point. But I just got busy. And for that same reason, I was doing so much shit and producing and rapping and doing features and beats and pressing records for other people and running around doing all that, so it was hard to focus on myself. Like I said, on the side, I did work on one but it kind of fizzled out. And I just never got around too it. I was just kind of doing good doing features and stuff. I really didn't have the drive to do it.

So it wasn't until we got the idea to do the *Nineteen Ninety Now* album that I was like,

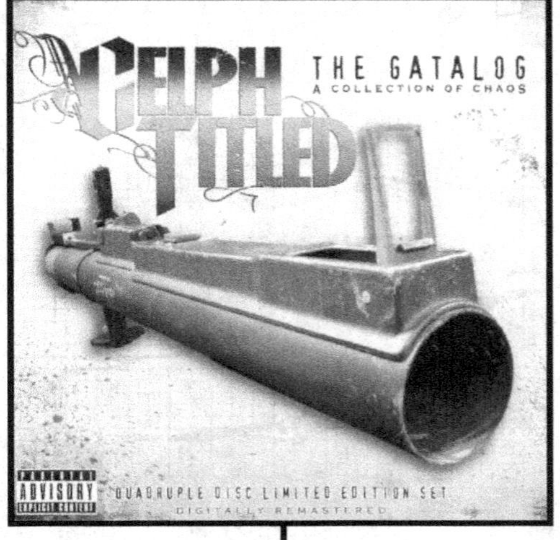

"alright, I'm gonna make this my debut album and it's gonna be crazy."

TUV: Was there a title or anything planned for the album that never came out? Like I know like the *'Fresh Prince of Hell's Lair,'* is the album title that I saw floating around, but that was after *Nineteen Ninety Now*. Was that the title that you had in mind before?

CT: Nah, the original album that I was going to do was called *'The Rubix Cuban."* My first solo 12", the one produced by **45 King**, on the back of that, it says, "from the forthcoming album *The Rubix Cuban.*" I believe. I gotta look at the packaging. But whether or not it's on the record, that was the name I was going to go with.

TUV: That would have been really exciting and I hope that you do end up putting out those early demos and include some of that stuff as well. That Lost & Found type stuff.

CT: I can tell you that some of that did end up getting released. Like I'll give you examples. The song, *Nut Reception*, that's on the *No Place Like Chrome* album.

TUV: With J-Zone?

CT: Yeah, that was supposed to be from the *Rubix Cuban* album.The song *Heatspeakers*, from the **Demigodz** Godz Must Be Crazier,

CELPH TITLED
"RIGHT NOW"
PRODUCED BY
THE 45 KING

SIDE A:
"RIGHT NOW"
1. DIRTY VERSION 2. RADIO EDIT 3. INST.
Produced by The 45 King for 45 King Records
Additional vocals by Malibu
"ROOT BEERS IN YOUR FRIDGE" ft. APATHY
4. DIRTY VERSION
Produced by Celph Titled for
Conquistador Productions
SIDE B:
"IT AIN'T"
1. DIRTY VERSION 2. RADIO EDIT 3. INST.
Produced by Celph Titled for
Conquistador Productions
"ROOT BEERS IN YOUR FRIDGE"
4. INSTRUMENTAL
Produced by Celph Titled for
Conquistador Productions
All songs recorded & mixed by Celph Titled @ The Chrome Depot - NYC except for "It Ain't" recorded by Brenda Ferry @ Harmolodic Studios - Harlem, NYC
All scratches performed by DJ Crossphader for PhonoSynthetic Productions
All songs published by Rubix Cuban Music [BMI], except for "Right Now" published by Headtrip Music [ASCAP]
For info & booking: celphtitled@email.com
All songs taken from the forthcoming album - "The Rubix Cuban"
Executive Producers: Dave Walis, Lyvio G.
www.celphtitled.com
www.demigodz.com
BRONX SCIENCE RECORDS
RUBIX CUBAN
DEMIGODZ
BUDS
℗© 2001 BRONX SCIENCE RECORDINGS. Manufactured and distributed by Bronx Science Recordings, a division of U.M.M. Recordings, Inc., 630 Ninth Avenue., New York, New York 10036 tel: 212-378-8848 fax: 212-378-8853
WARNING: All rights reserved. Unauthorized copying, reproduction, hiring, lending, public performance and broadcasting is strictly prohibited.

SURESHOT AFFAIR EP. 1997/8. SURFACED ONLY RECENTLY. APATHY AND OPEN MIC.

that was from my album. The song *Floss Filthy* with **Big Scoob**, that was from my album. So I used a lot of these songs, but there still are some songs that never saw the light of day. I got a joint with **Royal Flush** that's like a banger… I did it back in '01. No one's heard it.

TUV: Okay, so *Floss Filthy* and *Nut Reception,* I think those are two songs worth pointing out. Those are two kind of fun, upbeat, and a lot less serious. I think even *Nineteen Ninety Now* ends up being a far more serious record. There's some hard cuts, and the tracks that aren't hard are more sentimental and personal. Not really 'fun.' Was that the tone of the *Rubix Cuban*?

CT: Yeah, there was a lot of party-type fun records like that. Real **Beatnuts**-y type vibe. Just having fun. Hardcore lyrics but over the top to where it's funny. Yeah, pretty much. The other songs, now that I think of it, the ones that didn't come out, they were pretty much on that vibe too. There were hard joints though like *Heatspeakers* where it was like a hard-symphony type beat or whatever. But yeah, it was a fun album. It was going to be just fun. Pretty much.

TUV: Yeah, like I said, I hope the rest of the cuts surface. I never seen that *Rubix Cuban*, on the 12" either.

CT: Yeah, I got that here somewhere… yeah right here. Oh yeah! It says right here, 'All songs taken from the forthcoming album, '*The Rubix Cuban*.'

TUV: During that time as well, when you're doing all the guest material, you're also working with Demigodz. You talked about getting linked up with Apathy, but how did the Demigodz come together? Beyond just you and Apathy.

CT: Well, Demigodz was started back in 1990 by a group of guys in Connecticut including **Open Mic**. So it was around before me and Apathy came into the fray. When I met Apathy and got to connect with Apathy, he was already part of that. So it was basically him and Open Mic, who I used to build with all the time, it was just me, Ap and Open Mic always chopping it up. They just brought me in.

We vibed. We were into the same type of music. They were feeling my beats, lyrics, every-

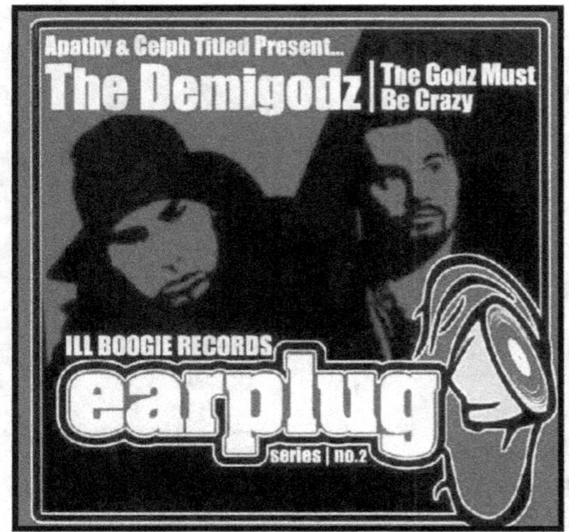

thing. So it was only natural that I got affiliated.

TUV: I think from the outside, *The Godz Must Be Crazy* really identified you as part of the Demigodz. [Side note: it's interesting how an artist navigates the identities of being a solo artist, and/or a member of a group. In hip-hop, and in Celph's case particularly, I think this straddling is particularly nuanced. Strong crew-affiliations yet solo is common.] You're so at this point linked in with the Demigodz crew. I think it'd be hard to separate you from that identity. When you started working on that album - did you sense that this was a [lifelong commitment?]

CT: Yeah, I was young. You gotta realize, that *Godz Must Be Crazy* that came out in 2002 or whatever, that's kind of later in the game in terms of my involvement. By that time I was at the forefront of the group. It was 'Apathy and Celph Titled' presents. You know what I'm saying? But initially? We were young kids. I'm talking 1997, 98 when I was first apart of it and I didn't really know everybody. When I moved to New York around that same time, that's when I got to really be in the mix and get to know everybody.

And at that time, you gotta realize, it's not that I was somebody like that... and neither was Apathy. So we just combined forces and something happened. It's not like I had a choice either. I had a bunch of people saying,

"you wanna be part of my crew? you wanna be part of my crew?" Like nah. These were fam, so it was like, "what else am I going to do? I'm on the come up... I'm trying to get my name known..." And back then it was good to run with a crew as you'd have a whole movement with it.

TUV: At some point here the production credits start to slow down a little bit and the rapping becomes the focus. [Today], I rarely see production credits from Celph Titled, it's always a guest verse. When did that become noticeable to yourself? That you were slowing down on production and just focusing on rhyming?

CT: Uhhh.. I mean..., money man. [laughs]. Really. It just got to the point where I was making more money to be a rapper. That was gaining more traction. In the beginning, when I was doing all that production for people, I was a serious emcee but nobody really... like you can shop beats, but you can't really shop yourself to rhyme. To hop on somebody's record to rap on it. Somebody will pick a beat and use it for their next single, but they're not necessarily going to hear you rapping on the street, like, "I'mma feature you..." So it was just a way to solidify my name in the industry.

Of course I love making beats at that time and I loved being a producer. But it was more so I had no choice to get my foot in the order but to do beats. That helped me transition more into being known as a rapper. Luckily that took off. It's much more financially appealing to be a rapper. You can tour... I'm not knocking producers, producers get money too, but there's just more possibilities as a rapper to get the bread.

TUV: Do you think the *Gatalog* helped make that more of a career move? Rather than just hopping on a homie's albums? Cause the stuff on the *Gatalog*, is all guys that you're pretty much close with. It's people that make sense. After the *Gatalog* your selling verses that are paying. Do you think that the *Gatalog* helped to make that transition?

CT: I mean, maybe… yeah. Cause I was known for doing so many cameos, I guess people wanted to have me as a cameo too. Everyone has their lane. Some dudes come in the game battle rapping and they get poppin' in that scene and they make a bunch of money being a battle rapper. Some dudes come in and their lane is to do real emotional stuff and serious stuff and tap into that lane… My lane I guess was being, I guess the crazy punchline guy with the crazy voice and all this stuff… Saying crazy stuff. And it worked, you know what I'm saying? But yeah, like I said, it made it harder to focus on my own shit when I'm just being spread thin trying to do all these verses for other people.

TUV: The battle rap thing is interesting as well. Because Apathy has his history with battle rap. Was that ever something that you thought of hoping into? That whole battle-sphere?

CT: Nah, I was never really big into the battle scene. Well, I liked watching some back then especially. Back then a lot of it was just so live. It was off the dome, a lot of it. It was over instrumentals, like a DJ switching up the beats. Kind of like **Sway** *5 Fingers of Death* type stuff, people doing that live battling eachother. So it was much more of a show. I loved it back then. But I was more into making records. I never even really liked watching rappers perform because I was like, "man, it don't sound like the record." I know that sounds crazy because, like "wow you can see them live and in person," but it sounds fucked up… So I was just into making records. To me, it was like a waste of time… At this time, I'm not saying now because it's very lucrative now, but back then I just thought, "man, this is a waste of time to try to write live

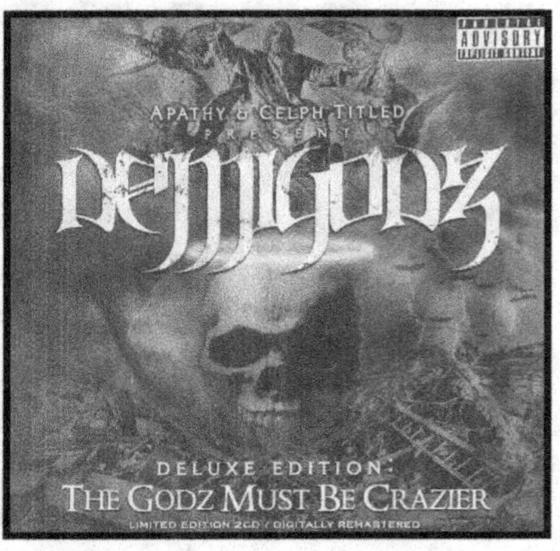

battle raps or sharpen my freestyle skills to win these battles. A lot of times you would do these battles back then and win like 200 bucks maybe. Or maybe not even win, just be judged to be the winner and shit. But yeah, Apathy was very very ill at that cause he was very good at freestyling off the dome. He was very good at totally chopping somebody down on stage based off what they were wearing…, everything. Just off the head.

Some stuff in the crowd, he'd make comments. He's just very very good at that. I watched him crush many many people.

TUV: It's interesting cause your style is battle rap, right? At least the style that you write records with, it would adapt so effortlessly into that culture if you were to take a swing at it.

CT: It would.

TUV: Is that ever something you thought of doing now?

CT: Nah, I respect those guys though. Here's the thing. The funny thing is, a lot of those guys came up listening to me. A lot of them have told me that. A lot of my punchlines and early stuff from back then, they came up on that. Cause of course, like you said, my style

is that style too it's just the platform is different.

I don't really wanna step into that. I never had a passion to do it. So if I was doing it, it would be really forced. It's not really my thing. I'd rather just let those dudes do their thing and I don't want to encroach into their world.

TUV: As a fan, one of my favourite CDs that you put out was that *No Place Like Chrome* with Apathy, the record with the *Nut Reception* track on it. However, when I first heard it, as much as I love songs like 'The Sound of the Clap,' and the other songs that you had with Apathy, I couldn't help but be a little bit disappointed that it didn't really feel like an Apathy and Celph Titled project. But rather just a compilation of songs with some of yours and some of his. And then a couple that had both of you on it. Do you think we could ever see like an Apathy and Celph Titled CD where the two of you are trading verses or trading bars. Like *Presidents Wife* JMT shit?

CT: I mean, we had started on something like that back in like 2012. It was called *Will Sing for Vengeance*. We're definitely going to revisit that. Right now, the biggest thing I gotta do is get a project out for me. So I'm working on that. And Apathy has a new album coming out as well. But we're definitely going to do that - come back around. After I get my project out. And as far as *No Place Like Chrome?* You're exactly right. You can tell from listening to it that it was like a compilation of songs we had. I have super respect and much love, there's this guy from the UK named **DJ Yoda**. He's a very well renowned, especially in the UK, but he's a world renown DJ. And he actually had headed a subsidiary of **Sanctuary Music Group** in the UK that quarted us for that album.

It was hard, we were doing so much stuff at the time. Like Army of the Pharaohs, and Demigodz and all this stuff... And Apathy had been signed to Atlantic at that period of time so he's running around. It just got so hard for us to stick together where it kind of got to the point where the label was like, "yo, if you guys don't turn in something by this date…" They had given us advance money, so it was like, "if we don't get a master by this date, you're gonna have to owe us back the money." And rightfully so. You know what I'm saying? So we just kind of scrambled to put joints together and what's what it became.

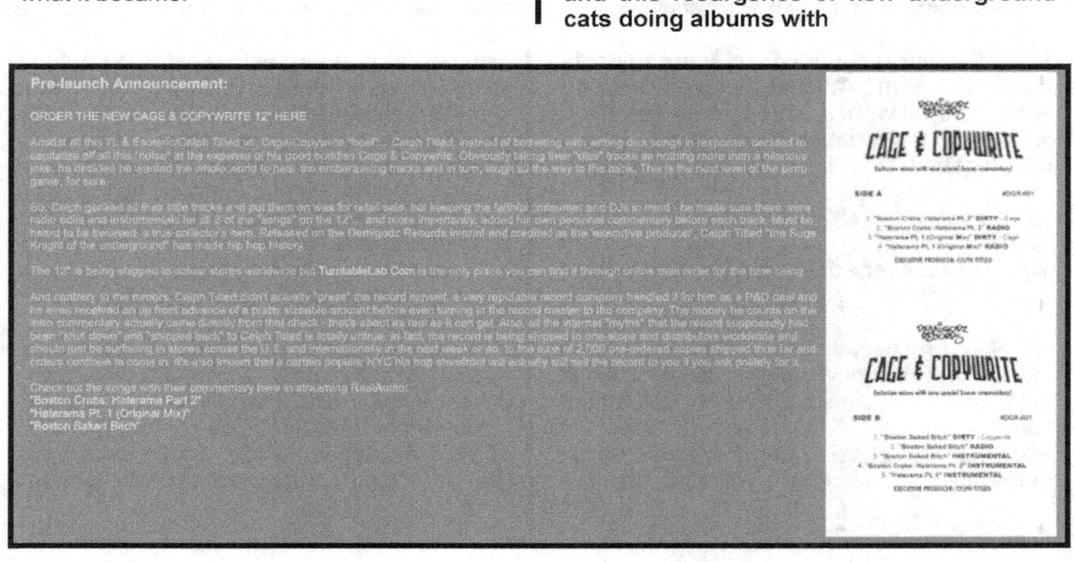

Even though a lot of people love that album and say, "that's my favourite!" this and that.

TUV: They're great songs, it just doesn't feel like you and Apathy.

CT: Right, they were great songs. It was just some songs were his and some songs were mine. That's just how we had to do it. I had just got back to Tampa at that time and he was in Connecticut. So it was hard to link up and work on shit, so that's how that came to be.

But yeah, it's not like they were throw away songs. They just weren't collaboration songs.

TUV: Moving forward a bit. I was a bit surprised when I heard the idea for the album with Buckwild. *Nineteen Ninety Now.* The idea that you got Buckwild to provide old beats that he did in the 90s that weren't necessarily throw-away beats but hadn't seen the night of day. The pairing though seemed really odd and out of your camp. Over the recent years, you have Apathy doing the album with O.C., and this resurgence of new underground cats doing albums with

---

legends… But at the time I hadn't really seen that. DJ Muggs I guess had his verses series. But even that seemed a little bit more 'in camp.' How did you get Buckwild involved in the project? And how did this idea get floated around that he was going to provide all these old beats? Cause even then, you didn't see Buckwild dropping albums. Now he does more work in the modern underground scene. But that wasn't the case then. How did that album come together?

CT: That came together through **DL**. From **No Sleep Recordings.** He was working with Buckwild at the time, doing some management stuff and helping him with some projects and I was dealing with DL as well. So just as we were talking, he was like, "yeah, I'm working with Buck…" And I asked, "yo, does he have old stuff?" Like first we were looking for old unreleased joints just as fans… But we found out he had a bunch of old discs. I was like, "yo!" And we came up with this idea to make this project. Of taking these unreleased vintage 90s beats and making them new songs… So he ran it by him and he was with it. He was familiar with my name, so it was a no brainer pretty much.

And we all still had to put a lot of work into refining it, but it was just a dope idea. Like, "yeah, these beats are already done basically…" So yeah, that's how that happened. That was just the connection. And ever since then, me and Buck have been tight. We still plan on working on stuff.

TUV: That's really dope. The bonus disc that was released with that album, 'Nineteen Ninety More…' It had the song, *Bucks Four Course Meal.* That obviously carried over from *Primo's Four Course Meal.* That was one of the favourites off of the album. For those unfamiliar with the song, it's basically the same as *Primo's Four Course Meal.* Taking these classic beats from both producers, four beats on each record, and it's you rapping over all four beats effortlessly and seamlessly. For *Primo's Four Course Meal,* I imagine that was just an experiment, but why the decision to carry that over to a series for Buckwild beats?

CT: The 'Buck's Four Course Meal,' was just promo material to help push the album. Like it was something we gave out for free. But of course, for people who wanted it on CD or whatever, we put it on that CD. But yeah, it was just an idea from flipping that. Cause 'Primo's Four Course Meal,' was like a real popular joint that people liked from me. So I was just like aight, let's just take that idea and do it with

Buckwild beats. That's really all that was. But I'm definitely... Actually I have it written, but whenever I do put out *The Gatalog* 2, best believe there's going to be a *Primo's Four Course Meal* part two. So it'll be four different **Premier** beats.' Same type of song. So I'll continue it in that way. I don't know if I'll do another Buck one, cause like I said, that was really just a spin off.

TUV: So what is happening with that *Gatalog 2*? Years ago I managed to make a version of the *Gatalog 2* with feature material since the first one, and there was easily enough, even back then to make a multi-disc compilation. I feel like if you were to make a second volume now, it would be 10-12 discs... I don't think that's feasible. So how is that structurally going to work?

CT: I don't know man. That's really been the problem with compiling it. There's a lot of reasons. So, there's a lot of ill joints I did, right? But it's kinda like... I can't just bogart... Like back in the day with the *Gatalog*, a lot of stuff was just wild west. Everybody did features for each other and were on each other's records... It was kind of before the digital era and all that. I could get everybody's permission of course, but I can't just gank all these joints and put them on my *Gatalog 2* without working something... At least getting permission. And the other problem is, I did so many features as how you said, 'features for hire,' which is cool, and I did my thing on them or whatever, but sometimes a lot of those groups or the people I worked with, there not good... You get what I'm saying? I don't want to taint it. I'd have to like pick the best of the best of those type of joints I did. Because that's really a lot of my material. Yeah, I have a lot of genuine collaborations with people in my crew, Esoteric, and this and that... but beyond that? A lot of my stuff is just kind of up and comers that I got on their tracks. So it's kind of tedious to sort through all of them and track them all down and find the ones that I do want to feature on there. It's just tough. You know what I'm saying?

I don't want to taint it. *The Gatalog* if you look at all the people associated with it, and everyone I collabed with, is pretty respectful. I don't want to go to this one and it's like, a bunch of

This is a compilation I just made for Celph Titled, it's bassically a gatalog 2.0 I called "The Gatalog: A Collection of Mayhem"

I seperated it into 3 80min discs containing all his guest spots, freestyles, promos, and the like he has done since The Gatalog was released...

Peep it if you are a Celph fan, it's well worth it. I also included a disc of AoTP features that he has done.

people you never heard of. You know what I mean?

TUV: I totally understand. At the same time, when you buy the first *Gatalog*, you feel like as a fan, that you have a complete collection of guest verses. It doesn't feel like there's a whole lot missing. You may be able to dig and find stuff from like Equilibrium or whatever, but for the most part, stuff that's there is there.

CT: Well yeah, the only thing is of course I didn't double up on songs that were on other CDs. Like other compilations. So of course I had a ton of verses on 'It's the Bootleg Vol. 1' with Apathy, but I didn't want to double the put those on *The Gatalog*. *The Gatalog* was more of a companion, for like, "if you collect my CDs and Ap's CDs, between those joints you'll have everything. You know what I mean?

TUV: So yeah, it felt complete. You weren't disappointed or unsatisfied with the material in any way. And I think regardless, if it's 4 discs, 20 bucks, you can't really complain anyway. But at the same time, there's going to be a little bit of the feeling, of "I want everything." But I get it. You don't want to have a disc that's just watered down with a bunch of bullshit.

CT: Yeah, and that's no disrespect to anybody I did joints with. But I have to pick the best of the best. And even the best of the best is just hard. I may have a joint with **Vinnie Paz** and then the next joint is with MC Joe Schmoe. It's just hard to narrow it down. But I will put it together and I will try to make it the best quality as I can. I just don't know when.

TUV: Speaking of Vinnie Paz and Army of the Pharaohs, and I don't want to dwell on beef, but over the years we've seen the falling out of a lot of cats. Let it be King Magnetic, Kamachi, or Virtuoso, and the recurring disputes between everyone and Jus Allah. Without touching on anything specific, do you think that we can continue to expect Army of the Pharaohs projects? Do you think we'll just get a re-fined roster, or be adding new cats to it? And what about cats like V-Zilla and Lawrence Arnell, do you think they'll have more inclusion in future records? A lot of questions, sorry…

CT: Yeah, no doubt. I would hope so. Really, it's up to Vin-nie. He's the one who heads up those projects. When he says it's time to go, we all go and we get on board. If there is another project and he green lights an-other project, he's definitely going to have a couple new members. I can't say who, I don't know how Vinnie wants to shape it. But I know he probably has a couple cats from Philly that he might want to bring into the fray which I'm all for. I'm just about making dope music. Army of the Pharaohs is just such a talented collective of so many versatile rappers and veterans man. So it's a special thing man… But yeah, I'm ready to go any time I get the call.

TUV: How do you feel about contributing to those projects? I'm sure there's not a whole lot of money in a 20-way split. I'm sure your ef-forts could go further else-where in terms of monetary benefit. But at this point - is it mostly just to expand your fanbase? Or to give back to

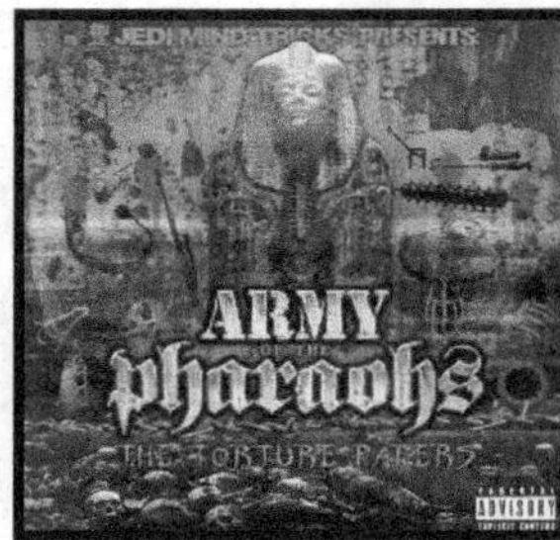

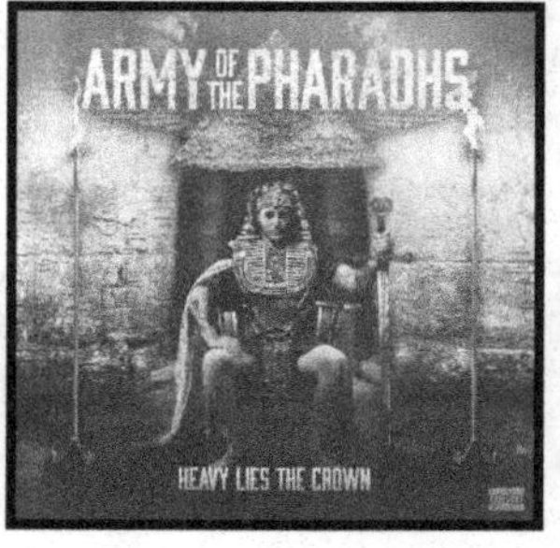

the fans you already have? What's your mentality behind putting work into these projects?

CT: I mean, as far as money goes with that… it's not as much about getting the direct, "oh I'm going to get paid for this record and this verse…" It's not really as much that, as those projects get a lot of traction and it just buzzes everybody up. So you get money in other ways. You know? Those albums come out and make everybody hot. You could tour, there's hits off of those that you can do your parts too at your shows… So it helps. It's not a direct check but you can make money from people buying features, people booking you, people buying merch. Those projects just help keep you hot. So yeah, I love doing them for that purpose. And it's never really an issue about money on doing those.

TUV: I want to talk about the new album. Let it be the *Fresh Prince of Hell's Lair,* or whatever you plan on titling it as of now, because I know that title was around almost 10 years ago. But whatever the new solo project it is that you're working on - what can we expect from this record? And I know there's been ten-tative release dates over the years, well, not exact dates, but like, "coming next year," or "first quarter of this year…" or whatever it ends up being. But do we have any new update on what's going on with that project?

CT: I mean, yeah… I'm not go-ing to call a release date. I mean, it's possible it could come out by the end of this year. But I doubt it. It'll probably definitely come out next year. But it's being worked on currently. And that's a lot to say, because there's just been a period of time here where I just didn't give a fuck. I wasn't doing anything. I had just lost my passion for the shit. I was doing other business stuff. And I just kind of debted the shit. Yeah, I was doing features here or there or whatever but I really didn't have the drive to make any songs.

So I got back into it. And yeah, *The Fresh Prince of Hell's Lair,* that fizzled out. I didn't want to keep the name because it was just one of those things where it's kind of tainted… People have such an expectation for it after hearing the name for so many years. And then it'll come out and not even be what I originally had in mind for it. Cause it would have got changed around so much that it just wouldn't… It's a great name. And shit, maybe I'll make a fucking song called that, or make a t-shirt with me with that moniker… but as far as the album title? It's dead.

But the album I'm working on now? It's all produced by Stu-Bangas and it's really dope man. It's really fucking hardcore. My lyrics are funny still, but it's very dark. It's very dark. And it's coming out really really dope.

TUV: Stu-Bangas. Great choice for producer, but I'm curious, why Stu-Bangas? And why not yourself even? You as a producer is talented. You have the ability. And I kind of thought the first album, before I found out about the idea behind Nineteen Ninety Now, was going to be produced by

yourself in a similar way with what Apathy is doing now. Why Stu-Bangas?

CT: Well, number one he got super super fire. Number two, it's also just a matter of time and effort. Yeah, I could make crazy dark bangers all day, but it's just a time issue. It's already this bad, that I don't have more material… If I was just like, "okay, let's buckle down, I'm just going to produce and mix and do everything…" it'll never get done. So I just got to be honest with myself and be like, "yeah, I have classic beats I'm sitting on, and classic fucking samples I haven't used, but I just can't… I can't do it." I need somebody else doing the other workload. And Stu makes beats that I would have made. He'll send a beat and I'll be like, "God damn. I would have made this. If I heard this sample, I would have made it and done it just like this." So it's just natural in terms of sound.

As far as what I'd be doing right now? It'd sound a lot like his stuff. So why not work with him?

TUV: You say that you could make these crazy dark bangers. Is that the sound for this album? Just that dark vibe? Cause Nineteen Ninety Now was not that.

CT: Yeah, this is not going to sound anything really like Nineteen Ninety Now. At all. That's not to say that the sound of Nineteen Ninety Now is bad. I'm just saying it's a different vibe. It's still hardcore hip-hop. But there's not really any jazzy samples and stuff like that.

TUV: Besides this new joint, is there anything else your working on? Is there another Demigodz album on the come up? What are you currently working on besides just the solo project?

CT: Umm, just the solo project really. I'm down to work. I'm doing stuff. Features for hire, and also stuff for my friends projects. I just did something for **Blacastan** and Stu-Bangas for *Watson's and Holmes*, the re-release of the original album. We did like a bonus track. Just stuff like that. Stuff for friends of mine and the solo album. Which is good, because any event that we do plan, a Demigodz project, or if Vinnie riles everyone up and we do an AOTP album, I'll have the time and energy to devote on it. But I'm just doing the best I can right now to get the album done.

TUV: Gotcha. And where can people find you? If people want to stay up to date in terms of social medias?

CT: Umm, well I'm fucking terrible at social media. But I could be reached on all of those. I'm on all those accounts. Twitter I don't really mess with all that much. Best way to get at me is email. Celph@CelphTitled.com. That's the way I will get a direct message from you.

TUV: Gotcha. For those listening at home, I will leave links for everything we talked about in the description. But again man, I can't thank you enough for taking the time out to speak with me here today. I appreciate it. This has been an interview I've been anticipating or high up on my list for quite some time. Since I started doing interviews. So thank you. And I'd love to speak to you again whenever you do have new material out. I'd love to keep this relationship going down the road.

CT: Yeah definitely man. And I appreciate you reaching out.

TUV: You have yourself a wonderful day. Thanks again, and yeah, I'll talk to you later.

CT: Alright bro, peace.

DATE: APRIL 18 2014
WHO: BLACASTAN
ORIGINALLY FOR: YOUTUBE (TUV)

TUV: Alright, welcome to The Underground Vault. My name is Alex and I am here with Blacastan! What is good Blacastan?

B: Yo what up! What's good man. How you doing?

TUV: I'm doing good! It's a pleasure to have you on here. I'm a big fan myself. I'm a huge fan. You're one of my favourite emcees. It's a pleasure to be able to sit down and talk with ya. And I appreciate you also taking the time out of your busy schedule to talk to me. I appreciate it.

B: No doubt! No doubt.

TUV: So there's a bunch of things I want to talk to you about today. But the AOTP project is the big thing that's really going on right now. I want to ask you a few things regarding it, but how did you get approached to join Army of the Pharaohs? As well as The Demigodz as well, as they were really around the same time. How was getting into AOTP and Demigodz?

B: First off all man, it's an honour to be associated with both teams. It's an honour. Some of underground hip-hop's elites. To be apart of that is just incredible, you know what I mean? It's natural man. We're all family. I did a record deal with Brick. **Ap** and I were friends for a very long time. I meant **Eso [Esoteric]**, me and Ap was tight.. I met **Vinnie**, I met **OS [Outerspace]**. And due to travels over the years, we just got close. I stayed close by. You know? Cause it was crazy just even being friends with these guys that I was listening too. And guys that I gave underground respect for their music. When I saw of underground hip-hop was through them. So it was incredible. Just building relationships with dudes that I respected as musicians already before we even came to the table with music. So we were friends man. It's one big circle.

TUV: Was there a call or meeting or anything that made you officially a member of Demigodz or AOTP?

Blacastan: The **Demigodz** thing was crazy. Ap and I were doing a radio show along with **Chum** [**Chum the Skrilla Guerilla**] and my man **Benny Shaik**. I think a while back, maybe six years ago now? Probably six years ago, maybe a little more... I had a song out, *The Life of the Tape*' came out on *Me Against the Radio*. My very first mixtape. Locally, 'The Life of the Tape,' was making noise, and I guess word got back to Ap and he was doing a radio show at that time so he reached out and said, "ayo, why don't you come down and be on the radio show? Let's talk about this joint you have and blah blah blah..." So I went down and did the radio show with Ap that first time and we really hit it off man. With a mutual respect for hip-hop and we listen to the same things. The knowledge of the music was just there. We vibed man... That one time I went down I ended up going back every week after that for like three years probably and became a part of the show. We just really hit it off and we became really tight.

A couple years went by before we even made any music together. It was just like we were friends. So naturally, before being officially apart of the Demigodz, I already felt like I was apart of the Demigodz. So he was like, "yo, you want to be down? You wanna roll with the Demigodz?" I was like, "yeah, it'd be an honour!" So he talked to everybody else in the crew and everybody was game for it pretty much. So he just said, "let's make it official." And one day he made an announcement on Twitter or whatever and there it was. I was officially apart of the Demigodz.

TUV: Speaking of the *Me Against the Radio Mixtape*. When you dropped the *Master Builder Pt. II* - you gave out 35 copies of the mixtape, first come first serve, to those who pre-ordered the album with UGHH. I got like 33/35. Are you planning on ever properly re-releasing the *Me Against the Radio* Mixtape?

B: Yeah, well I was actually talking about that to my man **ColomBeyond**. At some point I want to do it but it's so hard to find those original recordings. I don't even know where they're at. I know where a couple of them are and that's like so way back man. But I definitely want to do that and digitally remaster it, clean up the record... Take out the DJ tags and all that and really do it as an official, but a lot of that stuff is lost. But I'm definitely on the hunt to do that. That's something that I definitely want to do and let it out really official. It was mainly like a local release. We let it out and it kind of caught on. One day one of my homies were like, "yo! you're shits all over the place! It's all over the internet!" And I checked it out and I was like, "wow! my shits being bootlegged!"

That was like the best thing that could happen because people was paying attention. So right around then I started to take everything a lot more seriously. I knew that I had something that I could build off of and a lot of people really liked that project. That's what gave me the boost to go ahead and try to do something for real with the music.

TUV: So speaking on the Demigodz' *Killmatic* album and the AOTP 'In Death Reborn,' album, was there any difference going into those just writing style wise? Or your mentality going into those two releases?

B: I mean, the way how I always write, and if you listen, you'll notice… each record I approach a little bit differently. Cause I write records kind of based on the beat. I rarely ever write without music. So whatever the beat is, or whatever the beat is doing, that's how I base how I'm going to approach it. You know what I mean? If there's a different type of production, I'm going to approach the records a different way.

So if it's like a 'Murder Kill Murder Kill,' beat, then I'm gonna try to put myself in the mind frame of what the production is doing. Or if a record is sent through to me, and the emcees that are on it are doing something in a certain way, I'm going to try to match that vibe. So the production gives me an idea of where to go with it.

TUV: One of my favourite tracks that you mean was the verse you did on Virtuoso's *G8 Conference*. And I talked about that a lot last year on my channel. But it was one of my favourite tracks, I think I actually said it was my favourite song of last year, and just really really vivid imagery and I loved the concept. I think it goes hand in hand with what you're saying, playing with whatever everyone else is doing on the track.

B: For that man, **Virt** had an idea. He hit me up, and he was like, "ayo Blac! I got this thing! I think you're gonna sound really crazy on it. And he was all pumped up and shit. So he hit me up like, "yo you gotta get on this track." So naturally, the way that he was hollering at me for it, he had me pumped up. So I wanted to hear the record, and he sent the record through… and I'm not even sure if he had his verse on it already, I can't remember, but I remember really liking the beat. He was like, "yo, come out to the studio," and I drove up there man and when we got in the lab, we just started rhyming. I had my girl with me too which is crazy. She was in the session and I was in the session with Virt and man it just

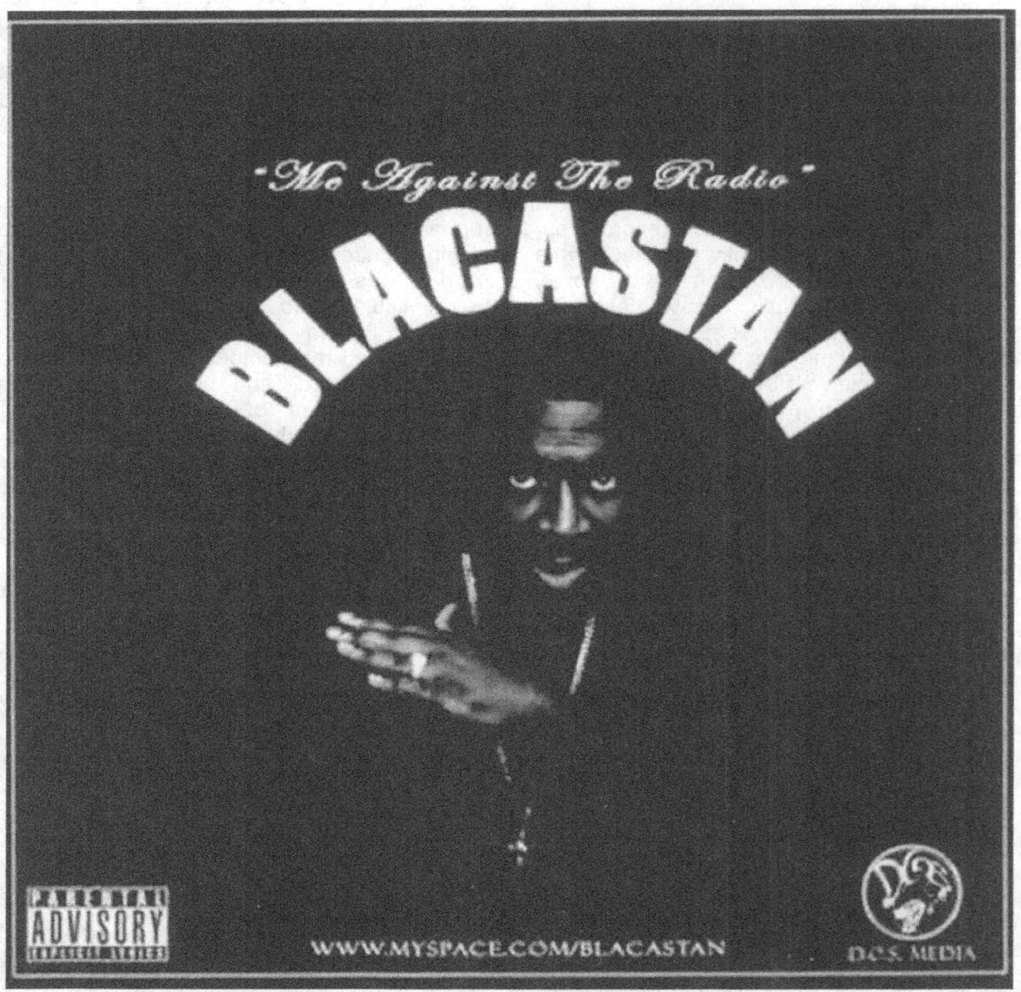
"Me Against The Radio"
BLACASTAN
PARENTAL ADVISORY
EXPLICIT CONTENT
WWW.MYSPACE.COM/BLACASTAN
DCS MEDIA

really flowed out.

TUV: Was Akrobatik's verse recorded for that already?

B: No, no. **Ak** had done his verse after. He did his verse after man. But I just remember, I laid… I laid like really, like 8 bars on the first thing and then I got stuck. On my first trip up to the studio I was able to get 8 bars out strong and I was really confident in those 8 bars. Like, "yo, this is dope!" and I got stuck. I kind of lost the feeling. He was like, "no worries!" and I was like, "damn, I really want to finish this." So I laid like 8 bars in the first trip up and I went back up to the lab with Virt like months after….

So what I had laid just felt totally different and I went back in and I started writing and he was like, "nah, you should say that… maybe you should say *that,*" and we really collaborated on that one man. I came back a couple months later and finished the verse. That's like really crazy to do that because the whole vibe and the feeling is completely different at that point. You know what I mean?

TUV: It came together excellent.

B: Yeah it came out dope.

TUV: Really fucking dope. One of my favourite joints that you did. That 'million dollar chandeliers,' line… that vivid imagery. You're known for vivid imagery… but with that concept in mind, you really took it to the next level.

With your relationship with ColomBeyond. He's kind of your main go-too producer. I know you're doing the album with Stu-Bangas which I do want to talk about as well, but you've basically stuck with ColomBeyond throughout your entire ca- reer, **and on top of that, ColomBeyond doesn't too too much work outside of your production. Can you tell us anything at all about ColomBeyond? As he's kind of a mystery producer to a degree.**

B: Yeah man, ColomBeyond… that's really him. That's really him. You know what I mean? He's an introvert man. He really doesn't socialize too much. And that's cool with him. I tried to get him to come out and do things, attend events, and he really doesn't do that man. He kind of just sits with a drum machine and the samplers and that's what he does man… When I met him, that was one of the things that kind of inspired me to work with him was that he always has a love for vintage machines. When I met him he was using an SP1200 with like sound modules and he had like an MPC2000XL. And at the time when I met him, all the software stuff was really a big deal. Everybody was really getting into software and he was kind of just varing away from that. The stuff that he was making was just like traditional boom bap. Where it was drum heavy stuff with the drums up front, you know what I mean? He was just doing it an old school type of way. I thought that that matched what I was doing because I stay rhyming in a vintage type of way.

That's how we hooked up man. We just got together and we made records… And this was like before I was even thinking about really putting music out or trying to really do this. Trying really beyond making music. So that's where the love [started.] We would just get in the sessions and we would just do this just to do it man. I feel like some of my dopest shit has come out with ColomBeyond. We're always going to work together man. He's trying to get more placements and all that, but he doesn't really care about any of that man. He just makes music. He just makes music that he likes man, and that's what we try to do. We try to just make stuff that we like and try to stay true to whatever.

Master Builder III is something that we hope to get done, so that we can get a complete trilogy with that and then close that chapter and just continue making music man.

TUV: A *Master Builder III* would be entirely produced by ColomBeyond as well?

B: I mean, I been discussing it with like **DJ Doom** and Stu-Bangas and ColomBeyond and maybe even some stuff from me on there production wise, but we want to make it like a full length and we want to feature Doom's, Stu-Bangas, ColomBeyond and myself. And obviously work with Pharaohs and just do as we be doing and just come with a fresh updated version of what we have been doing. Just seal that up.

We was actually thinking about making like a package with all of the *Master Builders* in it… But you know, all of these are just ideas man, but we really want to do another Master Builder.

TUV: A trilogy boxset would be really cool. I don't have the first one and the first one is pretty hard to find. The second one I have, the one with the alternate flashy cover thing, but I don't have the other. It'd be cool to have a reissue of all three packaged together.

I was talking to Zilla [V-Zilla], maybe last week as of now, and he was talking about a Blacastan and Zilla record, and he was also mentioning there would definitely be some ColomBeyond beats, maybe even entirely produced by ColomBeyond. What can we expect from this Blacastan and Zilla record?

B: I mean, to be honest, ColomBeyond and I went down to Texas and we went and we hung out for a few days with **Zilla** man, and we did a show, we was just chilling down there. Out of that mix man, we was probably there for four or five days maybe and we recorded like three records me and Zilla man. Man, the records are dope man. I'm not going to lie to you, I personally think the records are super dope. And we started to talk about an EP… at that time it just felt like a really good thing to do. I definitely want to do it. We're three records in. So that's something that definitely could happen. We just need to wait for the right time for it to happen. It's Pharaoh season right now man! Anything can happen. All I do is rap and rap and rap and rap. Man…

TUV: Especially with you and Zilla both being the two new members of Army of the Pharaohs, it would be nice to have a col-

laborative project to tell people what they can expect from you to both for those that weren't really paying attention to you prior.

B: Yeah man, Zilla's a monster man.

TUV: He really is, and the next album that he puts out too, *Martyr Music*, I'm excited for that. The single that he dropped with Lawrence Arnell produced by Skammadix… that was great. Even the work he had on *In Death Reborn*, was fantastic as well.

B: I would imagine that Zilla will be a lot more present on the next AOTP record because I believe Zilla recorded a few joints in that process. So I don't know where those records are but I would imagine that they might pop up on the next joint man.

And yo! Zilla's dope man. I don't think people… people haven't really seen what Zilla can do. I've been in the lab with Zilla and yo! he's a super talented dude… If you were able to be in a session with him and see what he really does, and if he played any of the stuff that he does, you would understand the magnitude man… He's that dude man. Writing lyrics, writing songs, whatever… Zilla's that dude man. Shout out to Zilla man, that's my brother man.

TUV: What about yourself in terms of the upcoming AOTP album [*Heavy Lies the Crown*]? The one that just dropped [*In Death Reborn*], had both you and Zilla. Zilla had a couple verses, and I think you had eight? Are you featured just as heavily on the next album? Or is that not really discussed as of yet?

B: Well, I mean… as of now? There's a few more joints in the mix that initially when this record was being worked on, that are still floating around. So there's definitely a few more joints that I'm on that are floating around. They might end up on the next joint. From what I've heard, there's some rotation going on for the next thing. But I'm just sitting back. I played my part man, so when it's time, I'm there… We're all brothers and we're all in this thing. There's a lot of us, so when it's time to showcase who's doing what, and at what time, that's who's time it is. So I'm happy that I've been able to be on over half of this first joint that's coming out. The next record is not completely finished yet, so it can go many different ways. *In Death Reborn,* is going to be crazy man. Whoever hasn't heard it already, it's going to be crazy… they're gonna love it.

TUV: It's one of the best albums of 2014 and you were fantastic off of it. Everyone performed and brought their A-Game. It was just impressive. And the production was high caliber, well done, and just well produced in general. Really captured your attention throughout the entire release. A great album. When I did my review, I had to say… you had some of the best verses off of the album.

B: I saw your review. I saw the review! The review was dope.

TUV: I appreciate that, I do. I want to talk about the album with Stu-Bangas. Now you've basically kept that under wraps. You really haven't talked about it too much. Really the least promotion I've seen for a Stu-Bangas album, and I seen a post maybe last year? Saying that that was intentional… But what can we expect from this Stu-Bangas album? When is it coming out? And what is the sound with it? Is it going to be feature stacked? Really what is this album?

B: I'll say this, the reason we're not really talking about it too much right now is because the Pharaohs record is all of our focus right now. Also Ap has a record coming out… So the Pharaoh's record, I look at that like "ayo, that's my record…" Know what I mean? So, at no other time would I be trying to put two records out at the same time. The Pharaoh's record, *In Death Reborn,* is my main focus right now.

I will say this though, the *Watson and Holmes* record is completely done. It's completely done and we're holding it right now. We're gonna set up a date but we don't want to drop it right now. We're kind of just holding back on it right now and when the time comes we're gonna put a super push on it. I love this record man.

I feel like I've grown to a certain degree on this record man. I'm writing kind of in a different space. Where I'm incorporating more hooks and choruses, opposed to stuff I did previously where I barely had like one chorus on like a whole project. On this one you're gonna see a lot of me trying to put hooks in there. Tie songs together, and write from different perspectives. Usually I'm heavy on the narratives, trying to paint pictures on every joint… This time I tried to lighten up. I have some different concepts in there. It's me, but it's me with a little bit of growth in there. It's gonna be different. You already know what you're gonna get from Stu-Bangas, and it's gonna be one that people are gonna love man.

We're branding something new. You know what I mean? Stu and I are teaming up and we're calling it that group 'Watson and Holmes.' You know what I mean? I think dudes are gonna like what we're doing on it. And hopefully we're gonna be able to put out more Watson and Holmes records after this one drops. It's dope though.

TUV: Can we expect an in house feature lineup or is it going to be pretty light on the features?

B: Well, on the features you're always gonna see Pharaohs. You're always gonna see Demigodz on my records because that's just family. If I'm doing the records, naturally I'm going to think about my brothers and who would sound dope on what. You know what I mean? That's how I approach it. So to me, it's no different than how the **Wu** did it in the 90s. Honestly. In my eyes, that's how I see it. Every Pharaoh record is my record. So that's how I see it.

If you go back to the **Doap Traffiking** record. You see like I'm featured on Doap's. I'm on the intro to **Doap Nixon's** album… and he didn't even rhyme on the intro! I'm on the intro!. So that's something like, 'wow.' You wouldn't see that. You'd think that the intro to the album was important, you would think that the artist who's album it is would be doing that, but that's something specific that Doap reached out like, "yo, I want you to do this." And that's why I look at his album like, "yo, that's my album too." Anywhere I pop up… Those are our albums.

If you listen to Machete *Mode* **[Esoteric & Stu-Bangas]**, I'm on Machete Mode featured on a song. And then on *Machete Mode* I'm just doing additional vocals on the hook. It's those little things that make this thing dope. Make this fun to me. Those little things make it classic. If you listen to *Honkey Kong*, I do the **Wu-Tang** skit on *Honkey Kong* for Ap… So it's those little accents right there. And I'm not even featured heavily on that album. I'm on like a bonus disc [*The Primate Mindstate EP*], and then I think I was on *Army of the Gods,* and that was it. And that was on like the *Gummy Bears* skit… So I love doing stuff like that. Know what I mean?

TUV: The very first time I heard of you was with *Blac Sabbath.* And I checked that album because of the Celph Titled feature. I'm a huge fan of Celph Titled and again, previously I wasn't familiar at all with your back catalog. And he was on the song *3010* with Esoteric. I had that track on replay probably for like an hour or so... but the more I listen to it, the more I loved you on it. Replaying the album though? The song that really blew me away was *Crac House.* Till this day it's my favourite joint that you've done. No question. 'Crac House' is amazing. What inspired that track particular?

B: I'mma be honest man. When I was growing up, it's no secret man... my mom was active in a lot of drug activity man. Growing up, those two kids on the couch that I describe in my mind, as I was painting that picture, in my mind I was thinking about myself and my older brother man. Just re-member being in the crib when my mom's was doing her thing. It's not like I was doing that to glorify, but to me, those records are coming from a real place... especially that song. I put myself in that mindstate again. And I was writing. I was try-ing to bring you into that picture. I really tried to bring you into that. When that's accomplished and somebody listens, they say "that's so crazy, I can see it!" It's the same thing that would happen when I would listen to like a **Slick Rick** or a **Nas** or a **Raekwon** or a **Ghostface** or whatever... I would see those images man. And I would think, "yo, that's so dope that I can see what he's talking about! It's like I'm almost in there with him..."

Growing up as an emcee and writing raps and everything, I always thought to myself that if I had that ability to do that, how dope it would be. "Up on the crack house, two kids asleep on the couch. They knocked out. Slog running out of their mouth..." You know what I mean? I tried to really paint that picture man. And I'm happy that you appreciate that man and that you felt that man. But that's like loosely based on real events. A lot of that stuff mixed in with a little bit of entertain-ment and people saw that. And it blows me away when you can catch my vision like that, you know what I mean?

TUV: You described it perfectly. You can tell it comes from a real place. When I introduce people to your music it's always through that track and I've literally had people just stop and say "holy shit, what was that? I want to hear more about this dude!" It's your type of vivid

imagery that you're describing... Let it be Nas, Raekwon or Ghostface, and I think you're right up there in that caliber, even if you don't have that 'legendary' status yet. Skillwise, with the greats.

B: Wow, that's crazy. I can't even take that compliment because these dudes are like the fathers of that yo... I remember just listening to these records man and just zoning out. Like, "wow." 'The Life of the Tape,' the inspiration from that I *Gave You Power.* Just listening to that man... **KRS**... I could just go on and on talking about hip-hop man. But like, Slick RIck... I just listen to this stuff all the time. I seldomly listen to new rap. I listen to all the old stuff man, and I don't know if that's a good thing. I don't know if that's a bad thing... Some people will probably say that you're stuck in the past or whatever, but that's what it is. I have no desire to listen to anything that strays to far away from the classic way that it's meant to be done. That keeps me in the classic mindframe. Especially when I'm working on music myself man.

TUV: It's working thus far. I would say don't change it.

B:Thank you man.

TUV: Speaking of DJ Doom. You mentioned him a couple times here. *Hey Young World,* **was one of my favourites off of the 'Temples of Doom,' disc. And you were featured off of that album a couple times as well. What is your relationship with DJ Doom and how did that come to be?**

B: Man, Doom... Doom is really my brother man. Doom is like my big brother man. Some of the strongest relationships that I've formed with people, I'd say in the past few years, or

the past 10 years plus, it's always through hip-hop man… I know that it sounds cliche man, but yo, hip-hop is such a big part of my life, that it's like all I do. I think about it all the time man. It's what I do. Know what I mean? Everything is hip-hop related. So when I form relationships, it's usually with people who share the same passion and the same passion for this thing that we got man. Doom, I probably known Doom, probably since 03' probably. 03', 04' maybe. Before I even did 'Me Against the Radio.' Me and Doom are both apart of this crew called **Defenders of the Old School**, so it's like 'DOS.' And I met him through them and we just kept a real tight relationship.

I heard his beats. It was kind of like the same thing with ColomBeyond. He heard me rhyming and we just gravitated toward each other. We really connected, you know? To where there's a real connection man. So we ended up hanging out, he would invite me down to his crib in New York or whatever and I would come through and we would chill, listen to records, listen to beats, he would cook out, know what I mean? We would just hang out. Making music just came naturally after we formed a real tight friendship. So we'd work on a record here, work on a record there, you know what I mean… and before we know it, we got 2-3-4 records. People like what we did. It was like, "yo, maybe we should do something man." And that's what the OC thing is like, many years after… We just dropped that.

People like that single with the *Passive Aggression* B-side. We're working on something too man… I never stop man, I'm always working on something.

TUV: That Defenders of the Old School that you were mentioning, do you guys plan on putting out an album under that title? Or a project, or EP, or mixtape, or anything?

B: Well, that was like the collective of a bunch of emcees man. My man **Rock Corleone**. Our **DJ Stress**… DJ Stress from Connecticut. My man **Lex Bug**, my man **Nick Vicious**… My man **H. Bomb** was done. And my man Winchester was down. So there was a few of us man. So I don't know what will happen with that. A few of the homies are still rapping and doing their thing. I'm kind of full speed doing

my thing. But it's all love. It's all love. You know, anything's possible.

TUV: Are you working on your next solo project at all? Aside from the Master Builder series. Like another *Blac Sabbath* album for example?

B: Yeah. Yeah. I'm definitely working on it man. But it's really not in the cards for the near future. It's something that could possibly be out next year. My next solo solo joint, I'm gonna really try to go crazy on it. That's my word man. So I'm going to really want to like focus this time and do that. But you know…

In the meantime, I'm just trying to get music out there. And stay present. And just, like I said, if you asked me… I'll say the Pharaohs record is my next record. You know, the thing with me and Stu is my next record. Whatever comes after that… that's my next record. I don't necessarily look at it like, "my solo record is this…" I look at all of these records like I'm giving it all that I got. That's one thing for sure. Every verse you hear me on, I'm giving it everything man.

And I'm treating all of it with the same level of respect like it was a Blacastan solo record. So I don't want somebody to see the Blacastan / Stu record and be like, "oh yeah, this is just a collaboration with Stu…" Nah, that's a Blacastan album! That's how you should look at it. Blacastan's on the Army of the Pharaohs record, nah, that's a Blacastan album. Blacastan's on Demigodz… That's a Blacastan album. That's how I look at it.

TUV: I get you. You're known for these concept tracks… Let it be tracks about stealing bikes, or the *Crac House* track, or the *G8 Conference,* or any of these songs that you've done. Have you ever thought about doing a complete concept record from beginning to end? Tying into the same theme?

B: Yo! Man… I've thought about it. And I've thought about it and yo, that would be a great challenge. It's one thing to write a joint based on a specific topic. That's pretty much… I can do that. But to seam together an LP that's all cohesively one concept weaved in… That's

very difficult. Throughout time there have been artists who have done it. **Sticky Fingaz** has done a record like that. **Kool G Rap** has done a record like that. I'm sure there's many others... I forget man. But I know that it's been done a few times.

That **Sticky Fingaz** joint was crazy! The **Kool G Rap** joint was crazy! If I ever did it, I would have to really make sure that it's just as crazy. But it's definitely a very serious thing to think a record all the way through like that. That would take a long time. It would be like making a movie almost.

TUV: I think if anyone can do it, you're in that field. Is there any feature material - albums that you're on - that we didn't get a chance to talk about already in the works?

B: I don't know man. The Pharaohs thing is what's happening right now. I have many records, some of the stuff never came out... some stuff is probably gonna come out. And that's another thing man, that I've been thinking about. I probably don't want to be that visible anymore in terms of just being all over the place. I kind of just want to settle in and

focus on just what I'm doing. Not be too visual, except for when it's time to do that. Yeah, I'm all over the place man. My main focus is *In Death Reborn,* right now. It's a beautiful thing. I'm officially a Pharaoh and this record is gonna stamp that man.

I'm honoured to be on a record with the caliber level of rhymers that's doing it. It's like playing basketball and just being on the court with the best players and you know that you gotta go in there and throw your two cents in there and help everybody win the game. You just got an all star lineup and you're just trying to get in where you fit in. If it means you have to throw the assist to make the basket go in, you just want to be there on the court, just to make sure it happens.

Then the Watson and Holmes is coming with Stu Bangas. That's already done. So it's already done. We're just waiting for the right time to throw a release date out there. The future is bright. We're just getting started man... We're just getting started.

TUV: I'm excited man. I'm excited. One last thing I wanted to ask you here, while I have

you. Is there a favourite from *In Death Reborn?* One track that's your favourite. Either something that you are on, or something that you're not on.

B: Oh man... Oh man... Yo, *Broken Safety's.'*The track that set it off... Paz gets on there and just... There's just so many. *God Particle,* it's crazy... I wish I was on that. *Azreal,* I think it is?

TUV: Yes! With Block McCloud!

B: That joint is crazy! It's always the joints that I'm not on where I'm like, "yo! this is crazy." Yeah man... There's just a lot of bodies. But 'God Particle,' is crazy. And I heard the beat, and the beat was so dope but I just remember feeling like, "yo, I can't even tackle this one..." I just felt like it was too heavy. The end result was so crazy, I was like, "woah." Could I have run the race like that? I probably couldn't run the race like that. You know what I mean? Cause the guys that were on that record were meant to be on that record, you know? And it came across like those were the perfect guys to be on that record. So in the end, that's how it is. You can sit back and you can still love the song. Everything doesn't have to be like a glory moment for each individual. You can just sit back and say, "wow, that's just an incredible song." Whether you was on it or not.

That's what's so dope about the album. I could have been on one song on the album and the album would still have been crazy. That's what's so dope about it.

TUV: You definitely listed some of my favourites. Another one of mine is *Ninkyo*

Dantai, which you were off of. Just a really really ill album. You've definitely explained my sentiments regarding the record.

B: *Sumerians... Sumerians* is nuts! Wait till kids hear the record man. I think a few kids already got the record because there was the pre-orders or whatever, but when it officially hits and people go in? When it spreads out? Kids are gonna love that record man. I love Sumerians. It's just crazy man. Crazy.

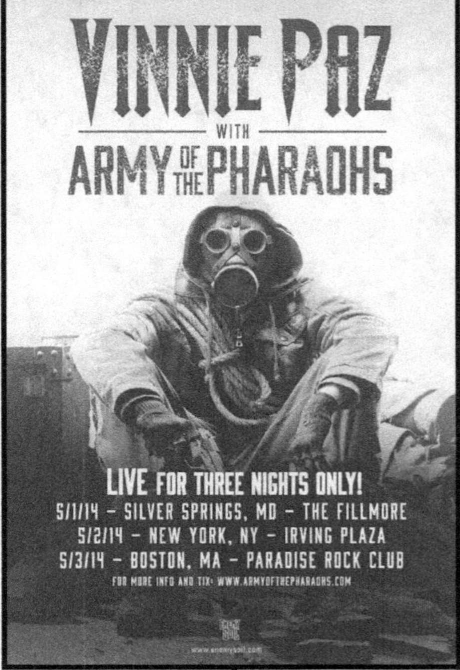

TUV: Prior to getting my hands on the advance, that was the record I was most excited about. Just the lineup. Being basically Demigodz + Vinnie Paz. I was hoping that was going to be my favourite. There's so many cuts to choose from.

Congratulations on Army of the Pharaoh's *In Death Reborn*. It does come out April 22 2014.

B: That's next week, right?

TUV: Yeah, today is the 18th I think. So it comes out on Tuesday, following Easter and 4/20.

B: Yessir. Yeah, 4/20 for all the winners! Easter falls on 4/20... That's crazy, kids are going to be smoking with the Easter Bunny man.

TUV: I really do appreciate you coming on. You're a favourite emcee. Demigodz is one of my favourite groups, as is AOTP. It's a pleasure to sit down and talk. Appreciate it.

B: No doubt man. Thank you for all the love. I see you. Just know, that we appreciate you dog.

Blacastan
04/17/80 - 02/20/22
"As we continue on!"

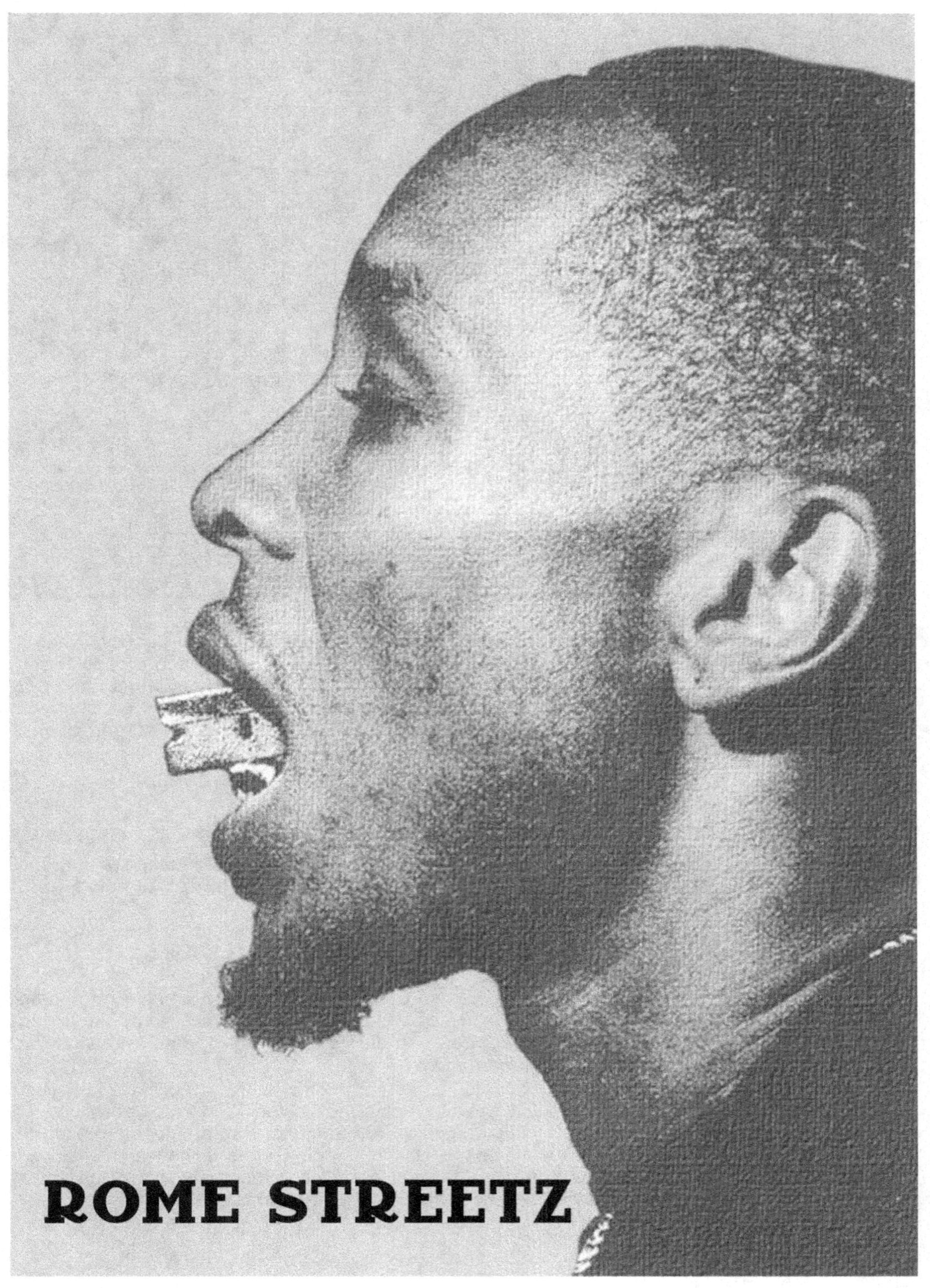

ROME STREETZ

DATE: AUGUST 1 2019
WHO: ROME STREETZ
ORIGINALLY FOR: YOUTUBE (TUV)

TUV: Alright, welcome to The Underground Vault. My name is Alex. I have here with me New York based emcee Rome Streetz. From New York City, dudes been making a name for himself in the last few years with appearances on Shady45 'The Come Up Show,' and just dropping consistent heat… what's good my man?

RS: Yo yo! What's good!

TUV: Ahh man, it's going good on my end. I can't thank you enough for taking the time out of your day to speak with me today. And to go through memory lane and talk to me here… I appreciate it.

RS: Yeah man, thank you for having me on the show.

TUV: Of course. So one of the things I'm always interested in is the history of an emcee. And I don't really know too much about you. How did you get into rapping and what era are we talking about?

RS: Well, I got into rapping just listening to rap. I grew up just listening to a lot of rap and then me and my friend we used to just freestyle and shit. What got me into rapping was that kids in my school were battling in the lunch room and shit. I didn't think they was really good. So I was like, 'fuck it, I can do this…' and I just went home and just wrote raps. And it's been on ever since.

You know, I was just doing this as a hobby but seriously? Taking it real serious? Probably like the last couple years I guess.

TUV: When you were battling around in the lunch room, dropping freestyles, what era are we talking about? Was that like 10 years ago? Or?

RS: The era was probably like early 2000s… Probably like 2002.

TUV: So you've been perfecting your craft for a while. Why did you decide to take it more seriously a couple years ago? And start putting stuff down?

RS: You know, I just started recording shit and it was just like, "yo, this shit is fire." You know what I'm saying? I just started putting it out there. Just building up. Doing local shows just around the city, showcases, open mics, and shit just started building.

I always knew I was nice. As far as rapping, I've always been nice with it. From back then. Everywhere I go, there's people rapping, I'm always like the dopest. I haven't really been in a situation in a cipher where it's like, "this nigga's way doper than you." I'm always like the dopest. So it's always been that for a while. So I always knew I had the ability to do this shit.

TUV: In terms of getting some of the material down, you're perfecting your craft on the mic - but in terms of production - who were you going too? Or were you dabbling with production yourself?

RS: In the beginning when I first started recording shit?

TUV: Yeah in the beginning.

RS: I just used to fucking take beats. Take beats off of the internet, fucking instrumental CDs, and just record over that. Kick my shit over that. And I just started meeting producers. I feel like this, as a teenager, I was always rapping and recording shit. I always had access to the studio. But it was just fun. This is before social media and the internet and all that extra shit. The internet was out but it wasn't like how it is today. So it was just pressing shit up, passing out CDs, doing it like word of mouth. Going out, getting in ciphers… But I wasn't really connected to nothing that could get me to that point.

TUV: One of the artists that you've worked with that I'm familiar with is Futurewave, and being from Canada myself, that immediately took my interest. Just curious, how did you and Futurewave hook up?

RS: How I met **Futurewave** was at a show. I met Futurewave through **Daniel Son** on Instagram.

TUV: Another Canadian cat!

RS: Yeah yeah! I fuck with Daniel Son. That's my guy. He came down here and I met him at a show. And he came back to New York. I don't think I met Futurewave that time, but the second time he came back to New York, I met Futurewave at a video. We shot a video, we did a show or whatever, and you know, we've just been corresponding ever since back and forth. Through Social Media or through text over the phone.

TUV: Have you been over to Canada yourself? Have you done shows over here?

RS: Nah, I haven't been to Canada yet.

TUV: Do you have plans to do so now that

you're connected to people like Futurewave, Daniel Son, etc. That whole kind of team?

RS: Hopefully I can get into Canada. I don't even know if I can get into Canada. We'll see.

TUV: Hopefully you do man. It's a good scene out here. We really love our underground hip-hop. Especially when you go to places like Toronto and what not, and it's close to the border, it's not too far away.

RS: Exactly. Toronto's not far. Hopefully I can get out there and do some shit man. I got a lot of supporters out there in Canada. A lot of people hit me up from out there.

TUV: The new project that you have out; *Noise Kandy*. This is volume 3 of the series. What's the idea or concept behind these? I understand the drug theme, but how do you separate these from some of your albums that you drop?

RS: *Noise Kandy* is just like an EP. The whole thing behind Noise Kandy was like, the first one started out - I just did a studio session. I had like won a contest and the prize was like five hours in the studio or some shit. And I just went there and recorded a bunch of joints. It was like, "you know what? I'm going to make this an EP." And then that just became the first *Noise Kandy*.

The second one, and really the whole thing behind it, is just like content to drop in between albums. That's just

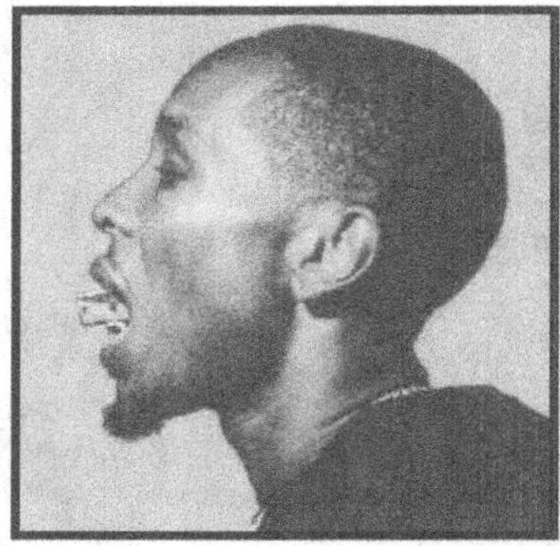

my series to drop while I'm working on an album in the period of the time where a couple months where I'm not putting out any music. Like, "damn, I haven't dropped anything for a while... let me drop this." So that's how the Noise Kandy series started.

The second one, that was the main idea behind it. The third one, I was working on an album, and I was waiting on a feature, so I pushed the album back and I was like, "you know what, let me just work on some other shit in the time." And for like a week I was just writing every day. Cooking up, writing shit every day. That's how the *Noise Kandy* shit came about. At first it was just like a couple songs. The first song is the shit I did with Statik Selektah. And that was like mad random too. So that was the first song I had, and I just started cooking up shit.

Creatively, there's no theme behind it. It's just me spitting bars. Just me saying whatever I want too. Kicking the dopest shit that I can.

My albums are more like... I approach my albums differently. Know what I'm saying? I always try to have a theme in mind, I always try to stick to certain subjects... It's more edited. I edit myself when I'm doing albums and shit. *The Noise Kandy* shit is no edit. It's just free writing.

TUV: Stream of consciousness type rap.

RS: Yeah! It's just raps. It's dope still, but that's just my whole theme for the *Noise Kandy* shit. It's just dope raps

over dope beats.

TUV: A lot of times when a hip-hop artist makes a series like you have with Noise Kandy, especially hearing what you said there in terms of it just being a 'waiting album' as we wait for something more substantial, often times it's considered a mixtape, and gets fuck all in terms of treatment. You've put effort into these projects though. In terms of pressing up physicals for everything you've done… Are you a collector yourself? Why are the physicals so important on your end in terms of some of these Noise Kandy projects?

RS: I would say the physicals… In the beginning I collected a lot of music. Before iPods and shit as a youth. As a kid I used to have mad CDs and shit. And I just felt like with my shit, I want people to own it. Some people actually want to just have it. There are collectors out there that want my shit. So you know, I do it for them. And I just have a thing, where

if the internet stopped tomorrow, would people have your music? What would happen to all your music? Would people still be able to play your shit? And if the answer is no, it's because you don't have anything physical for them to own. It's a product. You get what I'm saying? That's just the thing behind it…

TUV: You say the *Noise Kandy* stuff is just to tie us over till another album. So I imagine you're working on a current album right now. What's the game plan for you in teas an artist, what's the game plan that you're working on? Can you detail that with any depth?

RS: I think the game plan is just to keep dropping dope shit. My next album, I don't really want to give it away too much, know what I'm saying? But I got some shit in the works that's dope. With someone that I've been working with for a long time. Someone who is like one of my favourite producers. Me and him got something. It's with **The Artivist**.

If you've ever heard of this producer named The Artivist, me and him have a project coming.

TUV: Dope. Is that supposed to be coming out by the end of the year? Or?

RS: There's really no set date on it right now. It's not going to come out within the next month or two, I'll tell you that much. It's probably still going to come out this year, but I don't have a date for it. It's coming though.

I have a lot of music coming out. One thing I can tell you about is this album called *Big Turks*, it's with me, **Jamal Gasol** and **Lord Juco**.

TUV: Oh man, some fantastic names right there. Jamal Gasol is a fantastic artist and Lord Juco is great too.

RS: Yeah, Jamal Gasol's fire. Juco's nice. Yeah, we got that coming. That's dope. There's some other shit too. I got a lot of things in the works. I've just been making so much stuff and now that I actually sat back for a second and realized, I got a lot of fucking music. I got a lot of music out, but I probably have just as much music unreleased as I have out. Word.

The amount of releases that are on the way… It's a lot.

TUV: Yeah I'm a fan of everything that I've heard from you. So I'm looking forward to any kind of new material that you end up dropping.

For those listening as well, I will leave links in the description to check out the music. Where can people find you? What's your social media presence like?

RS: I'm everywhere. Rome Streetz. Rome like 'Rome Italy' and Streetz with a 'z' at the end. I'm on every platform. My music currently is everywhere. If you want to buy some physicals, you can hit up my Bandcamp, Rome Streetz, or you can hit up **FxckRxp** they have some of my vinyl. They have *Headcrack* on vinyl and they have *Street Pharmacy* on vinyl. Or you can hit me up too for signed copies. I do packages. I do a lot of shit.

More stuff coming. Spotify. iTunes. Whereever you listen to music at, it's Rome Streetz.

TUV: Thank you for taking the time out to speak to me. I'd love to have you on again in the future. Go through more stories.

RS: No problem man. Thank you for having me.

MONTHLY RATINGS

---

2 Eleven & T.F., Skanless Levels 4, Rap, ☆☆☆☆

A.I.G. & Shaka Amazulu the 7th, A.I.G. 7 Se7en VII, Rap, ☆☆

A.P. The Overlord, The Love Tape (Mixtape), Rap, ☆☆☆☆

AJ Suede, Ark Flashington, Rap, ☆☆☆☆☆

Amerigo Gazaway, City Hop, Beats, ☆☆☆

Andrew & Pagez, Smoke Chain, Rap, ☆☆☆☆☆

ArashiGenki x Bad FX x NOEL IS x DJ Robert Smith, Got The Message, Rap, ☆☆☆

Asun Eastwood, 7eventh, Rap, ☆☆☆☆

Beanies & Snapbacks, Beanies & Snapbacks, Rap, ☆☆☆

Big Dese x Mike Martinez, Lincoln Hawk, Rap, ☆☆

Big Sproxx, Duality, Rap, ☆☆☆

BK Bonez, Lucy, Beats, ☆☆☆

Black Milk, Everybody Good?, Rap, ☆☆☆☆

Blazewun, There's A War Outside, Rap, ☆

Bloo Azul & Spanish Ran, Bloo Moon 2, Rap, ☆☆☆

Bloodblixing, Sodom and Gomorrah (Gangsta Edition), Rap, ☆☆

Bokoya & Gianni Brezzo, Minari, Beats, ☆☆☆☆☆

Bombay Da Realest, Show is Over 2, Beats, ☆☆☆☆☆

Book$ & Chillon Daviz, Cold Fusion, Rap, ☆☆☆☆☆

Brainorchestra, Rituals, Beats, ☆☆☆☆☆

Bub Styles & MichaelAngelo, Behold The Andean Condor, Rap, ☆☆☆☆

Bugsy H. x Wolfman Jeckyll, Night Terrors, Rap, ☆☆☆☆☆

Buscrates, Control Center, Beats, ☆☆☆

Calculus , La Cosa Nostra, Rap, ☆☆

Capriisun, Calliope, Rap, ☆☆☆☆

Chino XL & Stu Bangas, God's Carpenter, Rap, ☆☆☆☆☆

Chung x Cotola, Chung Shui II, Rap, ☆☆

Clever 1 x Giallo Point, Gunz, Knivez and Nunchuckz, Rap, ☆☆☆

Cookin Soul, Whateva Vol. 5, Rap, ☆☆☆

Cool Calm Pete, LOST (Director's Cut), Rap, ☆☆☆☆☆

Crafsmen x Van Gunz, Grizzled Vets, Rap, ☆☆☆☆☆

Cuban Pete & BoFaat, The Year of the Rabbit, Rap, ☆☆☆

Curren$y & Harry Fraud, Vices, Rap, ☆☆☆☆☆

Curtis Roach & Illingsworth, Afro Bepop, Rap, ☆☆☆

Cypress Hill, Black Sunday [Deluxe] [Bonus Tracks], Rap, ☆☆☆

DamarTheEmcee & Cxrnbread Jxnes, 3 Summers (On The Run), Rap, ☆☆☆☆

Def Soulja, Moonlight Marauder, Rap, ☆☆☆☆

Denzen Davon & Jonny Onetime, Y'all Boys Got It, Rap, ☆☆☆

Dexter, Baby Steps, Beats, ☆☆☆

DirtyDef x DJ Kesti, #1, Beats, ☆☆☆☆☆

DirtyDef x DJ Kesti, #2, Beats, ☆☆☆☆

DirtyDef x DJ Kesti, #3, Beats, ☆☆☆☆

DirtyDef x DJ Kesti, #4, Beats, ☆☆☆☆

DNTE & Hagakure, Snoblo, Rap, ☆☆☆☆

Dookie Bros, Manure Music Vol. 2, Rap, ☆☆☆☆

Doza The Drum Dealer, La Cura Pt. 1, Rap, ☆☆☆☆

Drasar Monumental, Darker Than a Million Midnights, Rap, ☆☆☆☆

dread scott, Basquiat of the Bars: to Repel Ghosts, Rap, ☆☆

Drumwork Music, Drumwork: The Album, Rap, ☆☆☆

Emapea, Beat Catz Jazz, Beats, ☆☆☆

Emerg DA MC, Triple Blackness, Rap, ☆☆

Endemic Emerald, Renegade Soul, Beats, ☆☆☆

Enrichment, Different, Rap, ☆☆☆☆

Erv100 & Cedar Law$, Magic Hour, Rap, ☆☆☆☆

Esham, Purgatory, Rap, ☆

Fatboi Sharif & Steel Tipped Dove, Decay, Rap, ☆☆☆☆

FOHDH Matthew x Butter and Salmon, FOHDH, Rap, ☆☆☆☆☆

Fuego Gawdz, Fuego Proof Pockets, Rap, ☆☆☆

Funky DL, I Am Reuben, Rap, ☆☆☆

G Fam Black & A Dusty Cinema, Black Cinema The Fly Deathbed, Rap, ☆☆☆

General Jihad x Shaka Amazulu, By The Tongue (Jihad Bil Lisan) , Rap, ☆☆☆

Ghais Guevara, Goyard Comin' Exordium (Deluxe), Rap, ☆☆☆

Granddad Woolly, Oito (Blue), Rap, ☆☆☆

Granddad Woolly, Oito (Red), Rap, ☆☆☆

Grieves x Mouse Powell, WHY NOT?, Rap, ☆☆☆☆☆

Gryffyth & Pleigh Vader, Spur of the Moment, Rap, ☆☆☆

Gryffyth & Pleigh Vader, Spur of the Moment Instrumentals, Beats, ☆☆☆

Hazell Harris, Where Do We Go From Here, Rap, ☆☆☆

Heliocopta & Figub Brazlevic, Untergrund Platin, Rap, ☆☆☆

Hunnaloe & DVNTBEATS, My Brother's Keeper, Rap, ☆☆☆

Illah Dayz, Ponch'e, Rap, ☆☆☆

Imported Goodz, Siam, Rap, ☆☆☆☆

J.U.I.C.E., The Man, Rap, ☆☆☆☆

Jay Cinema & Jedos, Hell of a Life, Rap, ☆☆

Jeff Porter & Teathetruth, Stillustrious, Rap, ☆☆☆

Jelee, Soil, Beats, ☆☆☆☆

Johnny Onetime, Bobby Seale's Thoughts, Rap, ☆☆☆

JOHNNYTRA$H x Skip The Kid, Villains Always Win, Rap, ☆☆☆

Jose Cienfuegos & Pr0fit Diner0, Playing with Fire, Rap, ☆☆☆
Jules Clay, O.W.L.S., Rap, ☆☆☆
Jus, The FINISHED Mixtape, Rap, ☆☆☆
Kaimbr & Nathaniel Star, The Genuine Article, Rap, ☆☆☆
Kash Flow, Decorating Time, Rap, ☆☆☆
KenicRay x Burnt Bakarak, 84 Cutlass Supreme, Rap, ☆☆☆
Kheyzine, Hell On Heart Side C, Rap, ☆☆☆☆
Len Bowen, NTHN4GRNTD, Rap, ☆
Linkz Boogz, Sauce Talk 2, Rap, ☆☆☆
Lobe & Delicasteez, The Arc'ytect, Rap, ☆☆☆☆☆
Lord Juco & Finn, Company II, Rap, ☆☆☆☆☆
Lord OLO, Al Chimera, Rap, ☆☆☆☆
Lords of Ale, Weekend at Blazy's, Rap, ☆☆☆
Loveboat Luciano, Parole, Rap, ☆☆☆☆
LXVNDR & Tachichi, Found Money, Rap, ☆☆☆
Maddog McGraw, Shit Talking 201, Rap, ☆☆☆
Maestro Z, The Cookout Vol. 1, Beats, ☆☆☆
Mantis The Miasma, Mementomology, Rap, ☆☆
Matt Mars & Deadbent Inc, Dream Rotation 2, Rap, ☆☆☆
MC Roughneck Jihad & DJ Awkward, RAWK 2, Rap, ☆☆☆☆
McKinley Dixon, Beloved! Paradise! Jazz!?, Rap, ☆☆☆
Mickey Diamond & Sadhugold, Death Threats, Rap, ☆☆☆☆
Milkcrate, My Craft, Rap, ☆☆☆☆
Monday Night & Nitty Blanco, Any Given Scheme Day, Rap, ☆☆☆
MRK SX, Thank You 3, Rap, ☆☆☆
Napoleon Da Legend & J Scienide, Goat Vs. Sheep, Rap, ☆☆☆
Nas & Hit Boy, Magic 2, Rap, ☆☆☆☆
Nicholas Craven x Raz Fresco x Estee Nack, Gia… À La Carte, Rap, ☆☆☆☆
Nick Tesla, Nick, Beats, ☆☆☆
Nick Tesla & KGM Steezus, Don't Tes The Steez, Rap, ☆☆☆
Nivek B , The King's Regalia, Rap, ☆☆☆
Nonchalantly Zay , El Corazon De Oro, Rap, ☆☆☆☆☆
Noqh, Water to Wine , Rap, ☆☆☆
Noqh, Water to Wine (Instrumentals), Beats, ☆☆

Odd Pilot, Cabin Fever Chapter II, Rap, ★★
OT The Real, Red Summer, Rap, ★★★★
Page Kennedy, A Book of Pages, Rap, ★★★
Paranormal , When Art Becomes Ugly, Rap, ★★★
Patty Honcho, The Blaxploitation, Rap, ★★★★★
Pete Pluto, Black Jesus EP, Rap, ★★★
Premo Rice, Aye-Jae and King Joe, FOREVER TAPE, Rap, ★★★
Primo Jab & Hobgoblin, Jabgoblin, Rap, ★★★
Pro Dillinger x Wino Willy, Dirty Work, Rap, ★★★★
Psalm One & Custom Made, The Return of Bigg Perrm, Rap, ★★★★
Ransom x Nicholas Craven, Director's Cut 4, Rap, ★★★★★
Raw Poetic, Away Back In, Rap, ★★★★★
Raz Fresco, Pocket Operations II: Forty Seconds Only, Rap, ★★★★
Renelle 893 & Bay29, Off The Grid, Rap, ★★
Renelle 893 & Bay29, Off The Grid Instrumentals, Beats, ★★★
Rim, Rimbrandt Oil Based, Rap, ★★★★★
RJ Payne, Jigsaw, Rap, ★★★
Ronnie Alpha, Echoes of the Imperium, Rap, ★★★
Rove, Poke the Bear, Rap, ★★★★★
Royal Flush, The Sit Down, Rap, ★★★★
S18, Bronze Edition, Rap, ★★★
Sankofa, Iron Kofa Sharp, Rap, ★★★
Scam Musial (Rec Riddles & Capo), Scam Musial, Rap, ★★★
Sean Links & Machacha, The Iceman, Rap, ★★★
Sean Wrekless & Co.Z , Bitter Root, Rap, ★★★★
Sean Wrekless & Co.Z , The Bitter Root Promo Tape, Rap, ★★★
Self Savior $$, $$-Serial For Dinner, Rap, ★★★★
Shabazz The Disciple & Freestyle, Celestial Souljahz, Rap, ★★★
Shady Ray, Sheila's Boy, Rap, ★★★
Shaw Calhoune , Four Piece, Rap, ★★★★
Shottie, Death Occurred Last Night, Rap, ★★★
Silent Titan, Gold Chains & Therapy EP, Rap, ★★★
Skip the Kid, Fuck Ur Beats 2, Rap, ★★★★
Slumber Logic, Detachment, Homie and Only Detachment, Rap, ★★★★★

SoulChef & Uptown Squite, LUA, Rap, ☆☆☆☆
Speaker Bullies (Supastition & Praise), Art of Disrespect, Rap, ☆☆☆
Strong Creative, Dope Or Venom, Rap, ☆☆☆☆
Substantial, Adultish , Rap, ☆☆☆
Substantial, Adultish (Instrumentals), Beats, ☆☆☆☆
Teflon, 2 Sides to Every Story, Rap, ☆☆☆☆
The Alchemist, Flying High, Rap, ☆☆☆
The Allergies, Tear The Place Up, Rap, ☆☆☆☆
The Doppelgangaz, Hark Instrumentals, Beats, ☆☆☆☆☆
The Musalini & 9th Wonder, Don & Eye 2, Rap, ☆☆☆☆☆
The Palmer Squares, Junkyard Samurai 2, Rap, ☆☆☆
TheMellos & TrueCipher, Cocaine Crypto Currency Vol. 3, Rap, ☆☆☆
Titan Funk, Titanic Funk, Rap, ☆☆☆
Tonedeff, Deffinitions Vol. 3, Beats, ☆☆☆☆
Tony Tone, Sueños, Rap, ☆☆☆
Travis Scott, UTOPIA, Rap, ☆☆☆☆
Tree & Vic Spencer, Nothing Is Something (The Deluxe), Rap, ☆☆☆☆
Tree & Vic Spencer, Something is Not, Rap, ☆☆☆☆
Vega7 The Ronin & Superior, Sleep Is The Cousin, Rap, ☆☆
Vic Monroe, Immaculate Reflections, Rap, ☆☆☆☆
Video Dave & Controller 7, ArticulatedTexTiles, Rap, ☆☆☆☆
Vincent The Owl, Waiting 2 Exhale / 8 Ball [Digi-Single], Rap, ☆☆☆
William Bostick, Chessboard Billy, Rap, ☆☆☆☆
Willyynova, Godislove, Rap, ☆☆☆
Wun Two, Medalha b/w Montanhas Velhas [Digi-Single], Beats, ☆☆☆
Yokai Jem, Rap Tropic á lia, Rap, ☆☆☆
Young Malk, Head Over Hearts, Rap, ☆☆☆
Zoomo & Aasir, The Policy, Rap, ☆☆☆☆

BONUS: CHECK THESE OUT. FROM AN EARLIER ERA.

uMaNg & BBZ Darney - Lasting Impressions [2012]

Damu the Fudgemunk - Supply For Demand [2010]

Beneficence - Concrete Soul (2012)

MindsOne & Kev Brown - Pillars EP [2014]

K-Def - The Exhibit [2013]

Hassaan Mackey & Apollo Brown - Daily Breed [2011]

Supa Dave West - Beatboxing [2014]

Castle - Return of the Gasface (The Has-Lo Passages) [2014]

Esoteric - Serve or Suffer [2009]

Black Sheep - From the Black Pool of Genius [2010]

Dessa - A Badly Broken Code [2010]

Kyo Itachi & Ruste Juxx - Hardbodie Hip-Hop [2012]

MHz - MHz Legacy [2012]

Nujabes - Spiritual State [2011]

Viro the Virus x Snowgoons - Virohazard [2011]

Wax Tailor - Dusty Rainbow From the Dark [2012]

A-Plus - Think Tank [2014]

A-Plus & Compound 7 - Pepper Spray [2011]

Sage Francis - Copper Gone [2014]

Funky DL - Jazzmatic (Nas Remixes) [2013]

Gift of Gab - The Next Logical Progression [2012]

J57 - Wax Aesthetic [2014]

J-Live - S.P.T.A. [2011]

Marcus D - Retro'd [2012]

Masta Ace & MF DOOM - MA DOOM: Son of Yvonne [2012]

M.O.P. x Snowgoons - Sparta [2011]

P.O.S. - We Don't Even Live Here [2012]

Ugly Duckling - Moving at Breakneck Speed [2011]

Mello Music Group - Mandala Vol. 1: Polysonic Flows [2014]

Black Milk - Glitches in the Break [2014]

Blu - Open [2011]

The Chicharones - Swine Flew [2012]

eMC - The Turning Point [2014]

Emskee & E the 5th - The Marc Smith LP [2014]

Evitan - Speed of Life [2012]

Plug 1 & Plug 2 - First Serve [2012]

Soul Khan - Wellstone [2012]

Apollo Brown - 38 [2014]

Goldini Bagwell - Secondhand Smoke [2014]

Cityreal & Wes Mackey - Good Morning Blues [2012]

DC the Midi Alien - East Coast Avengers Presents: Avengers Airwaves [2011]

Epidemic x Tantu - The Solutions EP [2014]

The Funk League - Funky As USual [2011]

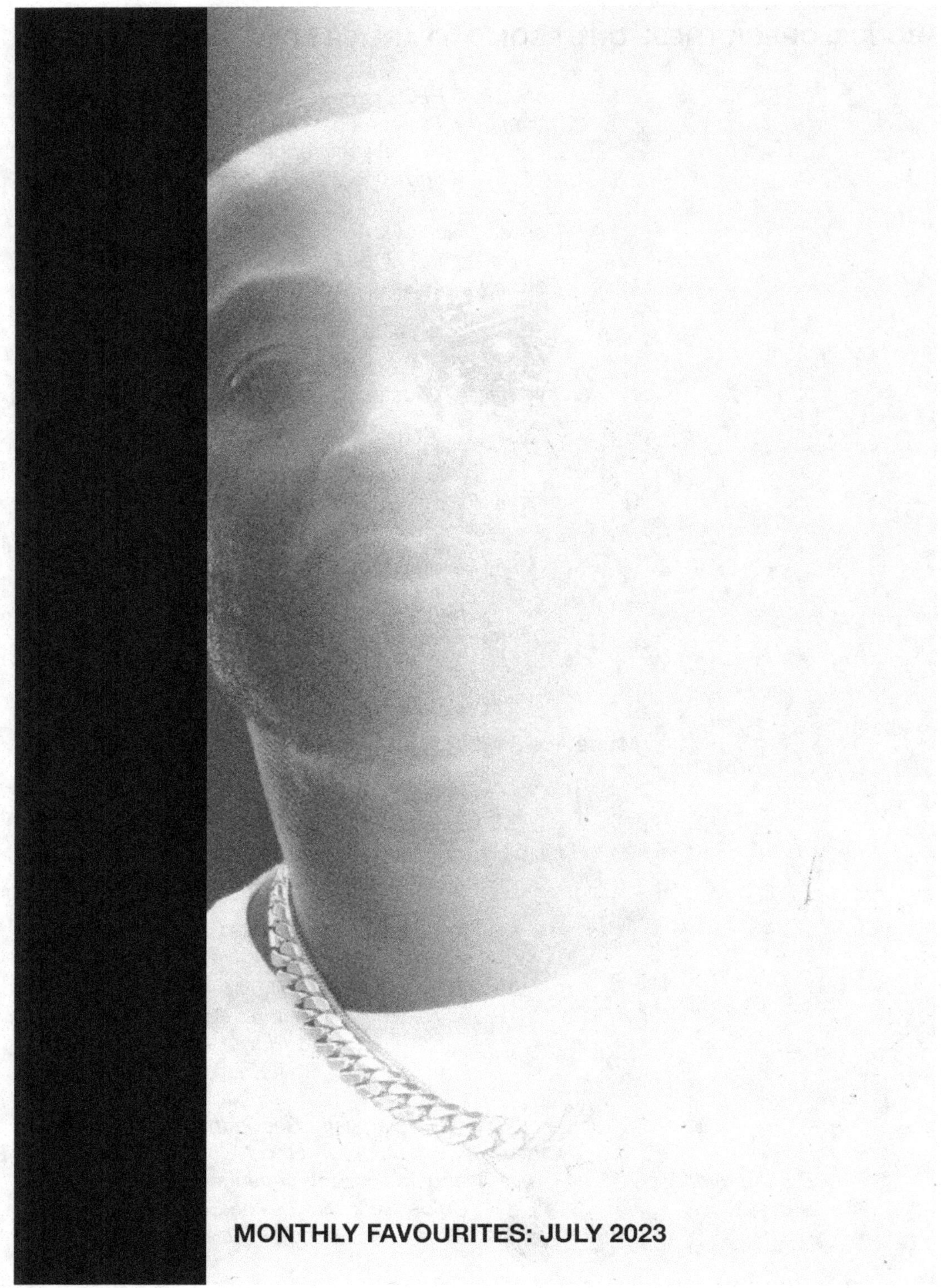

MONTHLY FAVOURITES: JULY 2023

Slumber Logic - Detachment, Homie and Only Detachment

Artsy, adventurous, loud, bombastic and dope. This has made me a real fan of Slumber Logic. Honest, thought provoking, great rhymes, great beats and stellar production. Not afraid either to take risks. A track like 'Red Riding' is a perfect example, an addictive non-hip-hop banger that ties ideas together. Strongly memorable and an experience of an album.

Rim - Rimbrandt [Oil Based]

Rim's back at it with one of his most cohesive, stripped down, 90s aestheticized rap albums of his catalogue. Similar to how Recognize Ali dropped 'The Return to Mecca' a couple months back - this is Rim's 'that'. If I'm in the mood for a Rim album, this will be the joint to go back to. Features from Sean Price, Ty Farris, Vic Spencer, Eddie Kaine, Pro Dillinger, General Steele and the like. Rough gutter rap shit with one of the nicest emcees out.

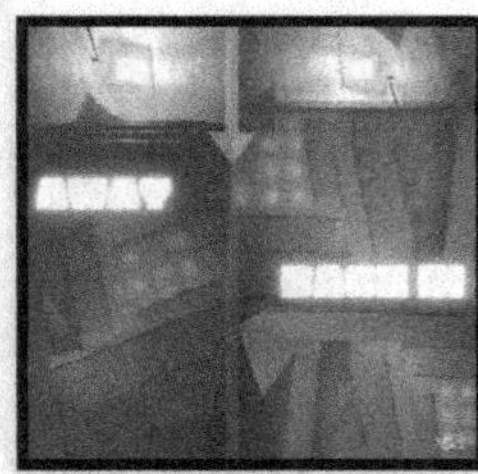

Raw Poetic - Away Back In

The 'Pat' album. Raw Poetic instills the help of P-Fritz to create 'Away Back In.' It's my favourite album that I heard in the month of July. Not as pretty as Laminated Skies, but just as moving. 'Sometime After Midnight,' 'Rehab,' and 'When the Mind Goes' are just some of my favourites. Raw Poetic's poetry is at center stage. Eclectically beautiful and composed. What. A. Gem. Raw Poetic is one of the culture's best auteurs. Find a quiet spot, pour a cup of coffee and sink into this one.

15. DirtyDef x DJ Kesti - Beat Tape #1
14. Andrew & Pagez - Smoke Chain
13. Rove - Poke the Bear
12. AJ Suede - Ark Flashington
11. The Musilini x 9th Wonder - Don & Eye 2
10. Bokoya x Gianni Brezzo - Minari
09. Nonchalantly Zay - El Corazon De Oro
08. Ransom x Nicholas Craven - Director's Cut 4
07. Grieves x Mouse Powell - Why Not?
06. Doppelgangaz - HARK Instrumentals
05. Patty Honcho - The Blaxploitation
04. Cool Calm Pete - LOST (Director's Cut)
03. Slumber Logic - Detachment, Homie and Only Detachment
02. Rim - Rimbrandt [Oil Based]
01. Raw Poetic - Away Back In

BOOK REPORT

PAUL'S BOUTIQUE by Dan LeRoy
331⁄3

BOOGIE DOWN PREDICTIONS — EDITED BY ROY CHRISTOPHER

MUSIC IS HISTORY — QUESTLOVE — ABRAMS IMAGE

MYKA 9   MY KALEIDOSCOPE

2Mex   Word Murder

RIDDLORE   BORN A VILLAIN

CULTURAL CRITICISM AND FAMILIAL OBSERVATIONS ON THE LIFE AND DEATH OF TUPAC SHAKUR — DATCHER AND ALEXANDER — Black Words

REBEL MUSICS — Daniel Fischlin, Ajay Heble, editors — BLACK ROSE BOOKS

the men behind Def Jam by Alex Ogg — the radical rise of Russell Simmons and Rick Rubin — OMNIBUS PRESS

Abe   EMERALD STREET   A History of Hip Hop in Seattle

6 'N THE MORNING — WEST COAST HIP-HOP MUSIC 1987-1992 AND THE TRANSFORMATION OF MAINSTREAM CULTURE — BY DAUDI ABE — OVER EDGE

The Creative Act   Rick Rubin — Penguin Press

Mael   HARLEM World   How Hip Hop's Super Showdown Changed Music Forever

LIVIN' LOUD   ARTitation by CHUCK D & The Near DEF Experience   Genesis

Emerald Street: A Histroy of Hip Hop In Seattle. By Daudi Abe. (2020)

This thing is worth it for the timeline at the back alone. 'Emerald Street' tells the story of the Seattle hip-hop scene from the late 80s until modern day. Seattle has continously had a scene. I've been most interested in the early 2000s - Elevated Elements, NAPS, 20604 - mainly due to the Vancouver connection. This book puts that scene into perspective. Pair the book with a deep dive into Seattle rap for the best experience.

Boogie Down Predictions: Hip-Hop, Time, and Afrofuturism.

Edited by Roy Christopher. (2022)

A collection of essays discussing how hip-hop intersects with themes of the time, afrofuturism. Ever wanted to have delve into thought experiments regarding Shabazz Palaces, Saul Williams, Deltron 3030 and the like? This book is for you. A bit difficult but well worth the exercise. Books like these allow you to appreciate the complexities of the culture and puts new perspectives on familiar art. For a brief overview of the book - listen to my conversation with the editor Roy Christopher via the New Books Network. It's good.

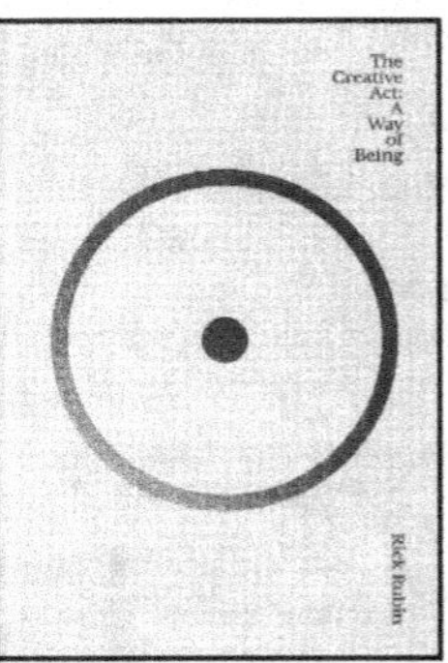

The Creative Act: A Way of Being. By Rick Rubin. (2023)

Probably the least 'hip-hop' out of any of the books here. The hip-hop artist writes general self-help / memoir formula at it again. This one is getting a lot of buzz. I can see why. It's easy to read, thought provoking, and looks at art as a spiritual adventure. I haven't read this in its totality, but hey... it's Rick Rubin's memoir. Plus he's been doing a hell of a press run, if you're in the market for this, you're probably already aware. I do wish Rubin would spend more time documenting some of his historical contributions. Maybe that's another book though. I will say, this hardcover-only print is beautiful. No jacket, just texture. It just 'feels' nice. Good for all audiences. Especially the artists community. Appeals to a non-hip-hop crowd.

6'n The morning: West Coast Hip-Hop Music 1987-1992 and the Transformation of Mainstream Culture. By Daudi Abe. (2013)

So before Daudi Abe wrote 'Emerald Street,' he wrote a book on the formative years of west coast hip-hop. Particularly interested in the rise of gangsta rap. I haven't spent as much time with this as I'd like, but it seems to be a good companion to texts like 'Original Gangstas' and 'The History of Gangsta Rap.' Quite detailed, expansive and full of information. Daudi Abe is clearly a writer worth following. I'm glad though he's transitioned to more esoteric scenes.

Born a Villain. By Riddlore. (2022)

Riddlore! So there's a few Project-Blowed books released recently. I purchased all these through LuLu and they came with similar prints. I will say, if you're gonna buy one (between this, 2Mex and Myka 9) buy this one. While the others opt for more poetry and thought, this one aims for history. Plenty of gems in here especially for the CVE fanatic. There's even a conversation with Dream Nefra about battling Eminem at the Rap Olympics in 97'. I hope more of these come from Blowed in the future - regardless of the *shape they take.*

Harlem World: How Hip Hop's Super Showdown Changed Music Forever. By Jonathan Mael. (2023)

This has got to be my favourite book out of the lot. A narrative on hip-hop's early years, but the story focuses on one event in particular: the 1981 battle between the Cold Crush Brothers and the Fantastic Romantic Five. Published by John Hopkins University Press, this thing dives deep and pays close attention to detail. Despite its academic approach, this beauty is a narrative. Rarely do we get such a detailed look at forgotten moments during hip-hop's formative years. Sure, the book paints the setting, telling the story of Herc, the Blackout of 77, etc. But once it gets going, it should be all new information even for the most die-hard of heads. Plus, we get citations! It's written accessibly, not too far off from your

favourite hip-hop journalism that's out there, but the citations truly put this over the top.

Word Murder. By 2Mex. (2021)

The shortest of the three recent Blowed books. 2Mex, of the Visionaries / Project Blowed, litters these pages with poetry, unreleased verses, and the like. For the most die-hard of Blowed fans. Spiritual, thought provoking, and at times beautiful. Open a page and be inspired. If you collect demo recordings, b-sides and rarities, and the like, this belongs in your collection. Otherwise, I wouldn't say it's essential in any way. That said, more love should be showed to 2Mex. Dude's a legend.

Music is HIstory. By Questlove. (2021)

I'll be honest, I haven't really dove into this yet. But hey, Questlove wrote another book. I think this must be the third or fourth thing I own from the cat on the bookshelf. This seems far more insightful than the cookbook, so I'll give it that. Questlove, taking a general approach to Black Music History, and seemingly advocating for the education rather than telling the story verbatim himself. Questlove always impresses with his knowledge, this is likely the same treat.

The Men Behind Def Jam:The Radical Rise of Russell Simmons and Rick Rubin. By Alex Ogg. (2002)

This is kind of the shape that I wish the Rick Rubin book took. This was published in 2002, and I think as of now, a lot of this story is common knowledge. Not an essential piece of literature, but if you're looking to build your Def Jam library, it may be worth a cop. If you haven't read anything on Def Jam though, I honestly think a run through of Dan Charnas' 'The Big Payback' is probably sufficient. Still waiting on that definitive Def Jam book. Perhaps one day.

Magnolia - Home of tha Soldiers: Exclusive Interviews with the Hot Boys & Cash Money Millionaires. By Mr. Harris Rosen. (2016)

Nothing fancy here. Short, large text, lower quality presentation. But that said, it's not the worst thing I've come across. I am a big fan of interview books, and let's be honest, this is a pretty underlooked and often undervalued movement in hip-hop. We often look at Wayne as an isolated iconic figure, but placing him within the local New Orleans rap scene is pretty cool.

The Making of Glasses Malone's Beach Cruiser. By Glasses Malone and Soren Baker. (2011)

Quite later than most stuff I'm interested in these days. Glasses Malone was a late addition to the Cash Money / Young Money roster. The book itself is largely forgettable. Small, amateurly written, and certainly skippable. Perhaps some value to historians of this era. That's it.

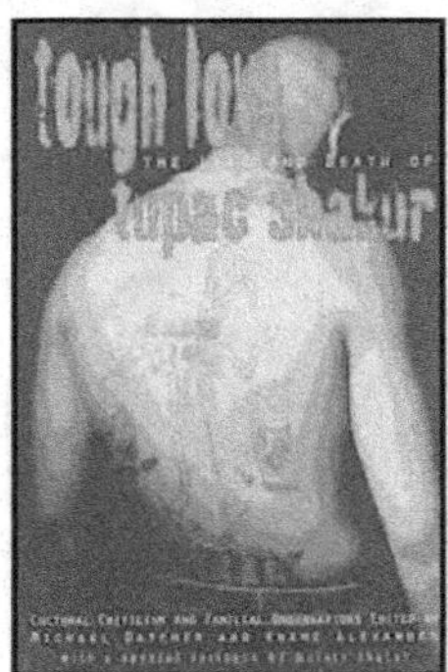

Tough Love: The Life and Death of Tupac Shakur: Cultural Criticism and Familial Observations. By Michael Datcher and Kwame Alexander (1997)

I frequent used book stores and always look in the music sections for hip-hop related books. I've came across plenty of Pac (and Biggie) stories over the years. But I've never seen this one. Published immediately following Tupac's passing, this is likely to have been seen as a cash grab at the artists expense. That said, what I dig here, is that this isn't an attempt to tell the narrative of Tupac's life. With significant work already done in that department (at least in today's time,) it's nice to see a different direction. Rather, this is a cultural analysis / critique of Tupac, and given the fact that this is written in the months following his death, I think it acts as a valuable primary source on the collective consciousness of Tupac Shakur. If you can find this (and there's a couple copies in stock floating around online), it may be worth the few dollars.

My Kaleidoscope. By Myka 9. (2022)

The Myka 9 book! Finally. This was the talk of the town last year upon release. And I get it - it's Myka 9. It's Freestyle Fellowship. It's one of those 'your favourite emcee's favourite emcees' type artists. Out of the three Blowed releases, I still side with the Riddlore text, but this collection of poems and thoughts is worthy of a grab. It's thick, materially dense, and I think has the ability to enhance your appreciation for the man's work. Die-hard heads already have this. I was sleeping.

Rebel Musics: Human Rights, Resistant Sounds and the Politics of Music Making. Edited by Daniel Fischlin and Ajay Heble. (2003)

A collection of articles on music, protest and politics. Not all hip-hop related, but thematically it often ties together. There are articles that touch on Public Enemy, and some hip-hop acts. I've enjoyed the segments I've read thus far. Centering culture in rebellion. Centering art as response to popular culture. Likely difficult to come across now. Not essential. Written in 2003. There's more modern texts on the topic if you're interested in contemporary scholarship.

I'm the White Guy: The Journey of Soren Baker's Life As a White Rap Journalist. By Soren Baker. (2011)

I keep seeing this on Amazon and finally pulled the trigger. Soren Baker has been around as a rap jour-

nalist for some time. He wrote one of the seminal texts on west coast gangsta rap, he's done the magazine circuit, and he's paid his dues. This small and rather inconsequential book, does tell a rather unique perspective: a white rap journalist, trying to navigate the space. Easily digestible within a day, and certainly not a must-have. But given my own place in the culture, I couldn't help but relate to the sentiments on the page.

Livin' Loud: ARTitation. By Chuck D and The Near DEF Experience. (2023)

How cool. Chuck D is a painter. If you follow the legend on Twitter or (I assume, other socials), you have likely come across his art. Really powerful stuff here. This photo book is a beautiful coffee table specimen. With an adequate amount of write ups and information to make it a well rounded product. But seriously, it's just a gorgeous book. And the art is great. Buy this.

33 1/3rd: Paul's Boutique. By Dan LeRoy. (2006)

I haven't spent as much time here as I'd like, but this was recommended as the best hip-hop 33 1/3rd recently, and I had to snag it up. Comparable to the Beastie Boys book? Probably not. But more historically focused than most in the series.

Have an LP/EP, book, podcast, etc. coming out that may be of interest to readers? Now accepting **7.25x10.25**, **5.5x3.0**, and **5.5x7.85** ads for the low-price of zero dollars. THAT'S RIGHT, FREE! I got about 20 pages of space I can utilize without effecting much in terms of printing cost. I don't want to sell ads to the culture, but I'm always down to help spread the word on dope art and hip-hop history projects. Send ideas or graphics to <u>tuvalex@yorku.ca</u>.*

* must align with the theme of The Underground Vault. If I've
covered your art in the past, you're likely auto-accepted.

www.ingramcontent.com/pod-product-compliance
Lightning Source LLC
Chambersburg PA
CBHW080853250726

48663CB00004B/446